Dining Out at Home

Dining

STACKPOLE BOOKS

Out at Home

Sophie Leavitt

To my husband Boris

Contents

Guide to the Recipes

8

Introduction

Dining out—at home? Of course! Anyone who delights in savoring exquisitely prepared food at a really fine restaurant can create this same gracious dining out atmosphere at home. In this book, you'll find the ways . . . many different ways to transform ordinary, everyday foods into mouth-watering gourmet dishes—with simple tricks such as adding a spoonful of brandy, a pinch of just the right herb, a dash of pepper, a special sauce.

Here, too, are easy recipes for preparing beef that taste the way good American beef should, with its natural flavor undisguised . . . for a succulent chicken in champagne sauce . . . for an old-fashioned apple pie, sweet and tart with a hint of cinnamon, and baked in a wonderful, thin crust.

There are hints, short cuts, time-savers . . . a simple formula for a sauce to give oven-broiled steaks a charcoal-broiled taste . . . the secret of using a knife to chop, cut and mince . . . how to keep salad greens crisp and fresh for a week, always ready to use. You'll discover the easiest, best way to prepare vegetables so they retain their inviting natural color and individual flavor. No soggy vegetables when dining out at home!

What's more, you can make dining out at home a habit whether you're on a tight budget or splurging for a special occasion . . . cooking for two or for a crowd . . . setting the table in an alcove or in a spacious dining room.

And it's all so simple! Who has time to grope through complicated recipes? Not you! Not I! Just a glance at each recipe here tells you whether the dish can be prepared in advance, how long it takes to cook, what ingredients and utensils are needed. You're told, too, which recipes freeze well, so that you can prepare a double quantity—one to eat, one to freeze. Each recipe also tells how many people you can serve, but you'll probably be asked for seconds!

Recipes which are used as ingredients in other recipes are referred to by their exact titles, so that the reader may find them easily in the alphabetical Guide to the Recipes. They are preceded by an asterisk (*).

In these pages you'll find my favorite recipes gathered through my lifetime as bride, wife, mother, career woman, grandmother. Here are dishes that stand out, that through the years have been enjoyed again and again by family and friends.

A dear friend complimented me one day by saying, "I like your recipes because they have romance in them." What did she mean? Was it because I have traveled from one end of the United States to the other? Was it because I've eaten gourmet food in nearly every foreign country? Or was it perhaps because I've talked and exchanged recipes with superb cooks—professional and amateur—all over the world?

I remember one experience in a small town in France. We stopped at a charming provincial restaurant where the owner was also the chef. And what a variety of heavenly food he prepared for us in just 2 black, old-fashioned wood-burning stoves—one for high heat and one for slow cooking—his own pâté, partridge on toast, a salad to dream about!

The salad greens were grown, tended and picked fresh by an ancient, contented grandpère in a tiny rear garden. My husband and I could not resist finishing every course down to the last delicious mouthful. To reward our appreciation of his skill, and to our dismay, our host whipped up an "out-of-this-world" soufflé, which we had to down smilingly, even though it almost sent us out of this world.

Well, that's all the talking in this book. In the recipes I've concentrated on the directions . . . no chit-chat, no talk-alongs. Each recipe is easy to follow and sure to succeed . . . with an extra goodness that's guaranteed to make your meal special.

Let DINING OUT AT HOME *become your constant kitchen companion. Whether you're a bride or a mother, career girl or bachelor, or just an experienced cook who loves to discover new taste sensations —this book can become your guide to adventures in good cooking and good eating.*

Sophie Leavitt

Good Coffee

There are many arguments as to the one best way to brew coffee. No doubt there isn't just one best way, but since we have received many compliments on our method, I'll pass it on to you.

First of all, buy the fine grind of coffee. Do not buy the percolator, or regular grind. This is very important.

This, too, is very important—always begin with *cold* water; not hot, not warm, but always cold water from the tap. Secondly, never fill your coffeepot right to the top; always leave room so that the water can percolate into the coffee. Third, do not fill the coffee compartment full to the top with coffee. Leave about an inch from the top so that the water will have room to perk over the coffee, and the coffee will have room to swell, thus giving back its fragrance to the water.

Never, never let the coffee boil over, as this will give the finished coffee a bitter taste.

Always clean your percolator thoroughly, and rinse well. Keep the top tilted, so that the coffeepot is never completely closed, but is allowed to air when stored.

Step-by-Step: Percolated Coffee

Whatever size percolator you have, use one less cup of cold water from the tap. For instance, for a 4-cup percolator, use only 3 cups; for a 6-cup, use only 5 cups, and so on.

Measure 1 tbsp finely ground coffee for each cup water, and 1 extra tbsp into the percolator coffee comparment. Place on high heat. Let come to a boil,

13

but watch so that it doesn't boil over—this is most important. As soon as it starts to boil, or "perk," reduce heat to low or medium low. Continue perking 10 min. Remove from heat. Allow the grounds to settle; remove the compartment of grounds from the percolator, and place the coffee-pot back on low heat; simmer until you are ready to serve. By following this method, you will have a rich, clear, good cup of coffee.

Another hint to keep your coffee from boiling over: put water in the coffeepot and bring to a boil. Now put in the coffee and turn heat to low or medium low and perk 10 min. It has no chance to run over.

a quickie

Melt-in-Your-Mouth Biscuits

cooking time 10 min (15-20
    for larger biscuits)
preheat oven 450°

1¾ cup bisquick
1 cup heavy whipping cream
little flour for flouring board

utensils
    ungreased baking sheet
    (teflon is fine)
    rolling pin
    smallest cooky cutter
serves 4-5

Measure bisquick into mixing bowl, stir in cream lightly. Gather together into a ball. Knead a second on floured board, roll 1 inch thick, cut with cooky cutter, place on sheet, bake immediately in middle of preheated oven 10 min. If biscuits are larger, bake 15-20 min. Serve piping hot.

You can substitute light cream if you add ½ stick or 4 tbsp butter cut into pea size pieces to the bisquick before proceeding as usual.

Always serve biscuits in a napkin in a heated dish or basket without a lid to keep them from sweating.

a quickie

Sour Cream Biscuits

cooking time 10 min (15-20
    for larger biscuits)
    preheat oven 450°

1¾ cup bisquick
½ tsp baking soda
1 cup sour cream

utensils
    rolling pin
    baking sheet
serves 4-5

Measure bisquick into bowl, sprinkle soda over it, add sour cream, collect into a ball, knead for a second on floured board, roll 1 inch thick, cut with cutter, place on sheet.

Bake immediately in middle of preheated oven 10 min until nicely browned.

fix ahead

Pancakes,
Swedish Pancakes, or Waffles

cooking time few min
  preheat griddle or skillet

utensils
  griddle or skillet, teflon
    preferred
  rotary beater
  spatulas
serves 4-5

2 cups bisquick
1 cup milk for thick fluffy pancakes or
    1¼ cup milk for thinner ones
1 stick, ¼ lb or 8 tbsp butter or margarine,
    melted
4 large eggs, yolks broken up with a fork
    and whites set aside
vegetable shortening to fry with

Combine bisquick, milk, melted fat, and yolks, being
careful not to overmix. Whip the whites until they
form a peak when you lift out the beater. Fold in
lightly. This batter can be used at once but is even
better if it sets 15 min or more. Makes wonderful
waffles as well; be sure to preheat the waffle iron.

For a thinner pancake batter, make as above; let set 15
min before you add the ¼ cup additional milk to
make thin Swedish pancakes.

Preheat the greased skillet; test with a drop of water.
If it dances lively, the skillet is hot enough to drop
small spoonfuls of batter to make pancakes the
size of silver dollars. When brown on one side,
turn over and brown the other side. Pancakes
taste best if served on heated plates.

Store any leftover batter in the refrigerator to use the
next day, adding milk to thin the batter. You will
have Swedish pancakes, so get out the lingon-
berries.

*The new teflon griddles or skillets are fine and a breeze to clean.
We do use a tiny bit of vegetable shortening to fry, as it adds flavor.
Pancakes baked in a hot skillet on high heat are best.*

17

Bee's Cheese Pancakes

cooking time few min

utensils
   griddle or skillet, teflon
     preferred
   rotary beater
serves 4

4 heaping tbsp cottage cheese
4 eggs, whites separated from yolks
4 tbsp flour
2 tbsp milk
about ⅛ tsp salt

     Add egg yolks to the cottage cheese; then stir in the flour, milk, salt. Beat the whites stiff and fold in gently.

     Fry on a hot griddle brushed with vegetable shortening. Make small pancakes the size of a silver dollar. As you fry, reduce heat as necessary to medium high. Serve at once, each batch at a time, as these pancakes are deliciously fragile and have to be pampered.

can be frozen

Waffles

cooking time a few min
   preheat waffle iron

utensils
   rotary beater
   waffle iron
serves 4-5

2 cups bisquick
1 cup milk
1 stick (¼ lb) butter or margarine
4 large eggs, whites and yolks separated

     Mix bisquick, milk, melted fat and yolks stirred with a fork, together, being careful not to overmix. Whip whites until they hold a peak when you lift beater. Fold in lightly.

     Preheat waffle iron before spooning or pouring batter. Bake waffles until they are as you like them. Serve on heated plates.

If you like thin crisp waffles, add ¼ cup milk to the batter just before baking. You can freeze any leftover waffles, then put them into plastic bags. Bake them frozen in a preheated 400° oven for about 3-5 min.

Around-the-World Blintzes

cooking time 15-20 min

utensils
6-inch skillet (teflon is best)
2 cloth kitchen towels
¼ cup measuring cup
pitcher
large skillet to fry blintzes
brush for fat

makes about 19 blintzes

BLINTZ BATTER
3 extra large eggs or 4 medium large
1 cup all-purpose flour
1 cup cold water
½ tsp salt to season flour
vegetable shortening to fry blintzes

CHEESE FILLING
2 pkg or 1 lb farmer's or cottage cheese, strained to remove liquid
1 egg yolk
2 tbsp melted butter
½ tsp salt
1 tsp sugar to taste

Make a well in the seasoned flour to put the eggs, gradually stir eggs into flour, mixing so there will be no lumps. Stir in the water to make a smooth batter.

Heat the small skillet, brushing on a little fat to keep batter from sticking. If using a teflon skillet, you will not have to use any fat. Pour batter into a pitcher, fill ¼ measuring cup not quite full, pour into skillet, tilting and rolling the skillet quickly to spread over the whole skillet, bake. Heat until cake pulls away from sides and is dry when you touch top. Fry only one side, do not turn over. Turn the pancake out on the cloth towel to cool. Continue until all are baked.

Make the filling by mixing all the ingredients together. Put some of the cheese mixture in the center of the browned side of each blintze, fold the top part over the cheese. Turn the sides in, fold or roll to edge. The blintze is made. Continue until all are finished.

Fry in a heated skillet with a little fat, reducing heat to medium high until all the blintzes are beautifully browned but not burned. Serve with the preserves of your choice.

a quickie

French Toast for Americans

cooking time a few min

utensils
  skillet
  rotary beater or fork
serves 2

2 eggs
4 tbsp milk
4 slices white bread, day old or older
¼ tsp sugar
large pinch of salt
about 2 tbsp vegetable shortening

Mix eggs with fork or rotary beater, add milk, salt and sugar.

Heat skillet with shortening on high heat before reducing to medium heat. Dip the bread into the egg mixture, fry until golden brown on both sides. Serve hot.

Bread Crumb Omelet

cooking time 10-12 min
  preheat oven 325°

utensils
  skillet
  rotary beater
  hot pads
serves 2

4 large eggs
salt to taste
1 slice bread, crust removed
½ cup milk
2 tbsp fat

Soften the bread in the milk with your fingers before adding to eggs, beat with rotary beater, season with salt.

Preheat skillet with fat on medium heat, reduce to low, pour in egg mixture, cook 1 min until the bottom starts to set.

Place in center of preheated oven 8-10 min; the top will brown. Remove to a heated plate, with the pretty golden brown on top.

20

eggs as you like them

Soft-boiled Eggs

cooking time 1-1½ min after water boils

utensils
    saucepan

serves as many as you wish

eggs from refrigerator
tap water to cover ½ inch over eggs
pinch of salt

Bring water, salt, eggs to a boil before reducing to simmer. Simmer 1 min for a 3-minute egg; simmer 1½ min for a 4-minute egg.

Another method—good when cooking with electric. Bring water, salt, eggs to a boil; take off heat and let stand 2 min for a 3-minute egg, 3 min for a 4-minute egg.

Tender Hard-boiled Eggs

Bring water, salt, eggs to a boil, reduce to simmer, simmer 20 min.

Cool under cold running water, set aside until completely cold before refrigerating.

21

Fried Eggs

cooking time 2-4 min

utensils
   skillet with lid
   small saucepan
serves as many as you wish

eggs
1 tsp water or milk for each egg
fat as needed

While heating skillet with fat, heat water or milk. Have lid handy before pouring egg in skillet. Spoon hot water or milk on eggs before putting lid on.

Reduce heat to low, cook 2 min for a soft yolk, 3-4 min for a firmer yolk. Remove eggs to a heated plate and sprinkle salt and pepper to taste.

This method of frying eggs makes a tender film over the yolk.

Easy Poached Eggs

cooking time 3-5 min

utensils
   skillet with lid
   slotted spoon
serves as many as will fit in
   skillet

eggs from refrigerator
2 inches water in skillet
salt and pepper to taste

Boil the water, reduce to simmer before adding the eggs. Cover, remove from heat, let stand 3, 4 or 5 min according to how you like your eggs cooked.

Remove the eggs with slotted spoon, season with salt and pepper, serve on a heated plate or on hot buttered toast.

If eggs have to wait, slip them into warm water. Be sure to serve on heated plates.

Shirred Eggs

cooking time 2-3 min
    preheat broiler

utensils
    skillet
serves as many as you wish

eggs
butter or margarine as needed
1 tsp water or cream for each egg

    Heat skillet with fat before adding eggs. Fry ½ min until a thin layer of white appears on the bottom.

    Remove from heat, spoon the hot water or cream on the eggs; then place them 1 inch below the broiling unit, watching carefully, as it only takes 1 min for the egg whites to set and the yolks to film. Remove, season, serve at once.

Vary this by decorating with some heated tomato sauce, catsup, broiled bacon or cooked sausage.

Scrambled Eggs

cooking time a few min

utensils
    skillet
    wooden spoon
    rotary beater

eggs
salt and pepper to taste
butter or margarine

    Beat lightly salted eggs with rotary beater until light.

    Put them in the heated, buttered skillet, reducing heat to medium high, stirring with the wooden spoon until all of a sudden, in 1-2 mins, the eggs start to set.

    Continue stirring until the eggs are soft, tender and scrambled, yet a little moist. The eggs will continue to cook after they are removed from the heat. Season with pepper, serve on heated plates.

If cooking on electric heat, move the skillet off and on heat so as not to overcook.

23

can prepare ahead

Rosa's Chicken Liver Omelet

cooking *time* 8-10 min

utensils
skillet
rotary beater
serves 2

6 fresh chicken livers
4 eggs
4 tbsp butter or margarine as needed
1 small onion minced
salt and pepper to taste

Sauté onion soft but not brown, set aside.

Cut chicken livers into quarters, fry gently in fat in preheated skillet 3-4 min until no blood shows. The liver should be juicy, not mealy. Set aside.

Beat eggs with rotary beater, season with salt, fry in preheated skillet with fat, adding the livers and onions, cook on medium heat, shaking and moving pan so omelet doesn't burn. Lift omelet to let raw egg run under to cook. When bottom is brown, not burned, turn over to brown the other side.

Serve at once on heated plate, adding a grind of pepper.

fix ahead

Stuffed Eggs

cooking *time* 15 min after
bringing to a boil

utensils
saucepan
strainer
bowl
serves as many as you wish

* 2 "Tender Hard-boiled Eggs" (see its recipe)
3 tsp unsweetened mayonnaise
1 tsp wet mustard
salt to taste
sprinkle of paprika

Cut hard-boiled eggs in half lengthwise, push the yolks through the strainer into a bowl, gradually stir in the mayonnaise, then the mustard. Season with salt, stuff the whites with the seasoned yolks, decorate with paprika.

24

Baked Eggs

cooking time 7-10 min
    preheat oven 375°

utensils
    small fireprooof baking
        dishes
    pan large enough to hold
        baking dishes
    saucepan

eggs, as many as you wish
butter to butter baking dishes
½ inch hot water in pan
1 tbsp tomato sauce seasoned with salt,
    pepper and ¼ tsp sherry for each egg
1 tbsp cream for each egg
salt and pepper to taste

Put ½ inch hot water in the pan. While bringing it to a boil, heat the seasoned tomato sauce before putting into the buttered fireproof dishes. When the water boils, reduce the heat to medium and put in the dishes with the sauce to get hot. Then break the eggs in. Heat the cream and spoon over each egg.

Place in the middle of the oven and bake 7 min for a soft yolk, 8-10 min for a firmer one. Remove, season with salt and pepper, serve.

This is a very tasty way to fix eggs, and it's easier to do than to read.

Stuffed Eggs with Sardines

Follow the procedure in *"Stuffed Eggs," (see its recipe), stirring into the strained yolks 3 mashed sardines, 1 tbsp unsweetened mayonnaise, ½ tsp Nance's mustard, ⅛ teaspoon dry mustard and ½ tbsp sherry, salt to taste. Stuff the whites as above.

Crisp Tender Broiled Bacon

cooking time 5-8 min

utensils
    broiling pan and rack
    tongs
serves as many as you wish

bacon—thin-sliced, bright color, not dark red, fresh-looking, not hard and dried out

The best way to prepare bacon is to broil it, as it does not cook in its fat. It should be prepared the last minute before serving, as bacon doesn't wait well. If serving eggs do them first as eggs keep better than bacon.

Arrange bacon on rack in broiling pan, place on second shelf from top of oven. Watch bacon as it broils, turning 4 times to melt the fat evenly as it broils. Watch it, don't go away.

When the bacon is crisp but not hard, which takes about 5 min, remove to paper towels with tongs, use an extra towel to remove fat on top before serving on a heated plate.

There is nothing worse than hard bacon except raw bacon, so remember the secret of good bacon is to stay with it, turning it over and over, removing when crisp and tender, not hard.

Sausage Poached in Vermouth

cooking *time* about 5 min

utensils
  small saucepan
serves as many as you wish

little tiny sausages (Mayers, Rath or Little Smokies)
vermouth to cover sausages

Cover the sausages in the vermouth and heat about 5 min.

These are flavorful and juicy and pep up eggs.

Fried Ham

cooking *time* 5-10 min

utensils
  skillet
serves 2

1 slice ham
1-2 tbsp butter, margarine or other fat

Cut diagonal slits into the fat around the ham to keep the ham from curling.

Heat the skillet, add fat (don't burn it), put in ham, reduce heat to low, brown nicely, being careful not to overcook the slice nor to use high heat, as it dries and shrivels the ham.

If you have a thick, tender ham slice, center-cut, you can broil it, brushing it with butter, being careful not to overbroil it, as it will become dry. Also if using an electric broiler, move the ham down, so it doesn't brown too fast.

27

Homemade Strawberry Preserves

cooking time about 10 min
after bringing berries to
boil

utensils
wooden spoon
large heavy kettle
qt heatproof measuring
cup
large mixing bowl
metal spoon
small screw-top freezer
jars, ½ pt
makes 5-6 jars

1 heaping quart cup firm, fresh, bright red
strawberries, washed in 3 waters, stems
removed with nipper after washing
4 level cups sugar
1 cup water

In kettle on high heat, make syrup of sugar and water;
bring to rolling boil, stirring so it will not stick or
burn.

Add strawberries to syrup while stirring with wooden
spoon, being careful not to crush them. Bring back
to boil. Boil on high heat or medium high heat—
no lower. Don't let it boil over, as it's very messy
to clean the stove. Boil about 10 min. Remove
from heat and test by dropping spoonful of jelly
on saucer. Place in refrigerator. After several min,
remove and tilt to see whether it has formed a skin.
If not, continue cooking another min; take off heat
and retest. Continue this process until you can see
skin. Usually skin is formed when boiled 10 min,
and the preserves are done, so don't overcook. The
time does change with the type of berries.

Use firm, not overripe, strawberries, as the firm type
contains more pectin and makes the best jelly.

Remove preserves to large mixing bowl, being careful
not to burn yourself. With metal spoon, remove
scum by moving it to the center and scooping it
out. When you have removed all you can, swish
small pieces of paper towels over top, and scum
will cling to the paper. Set aside until cold; do not

28

remove preserves until cold, as juice will separate from strawberries. When cold, ladle into small screw-top jars.

The best method of storing is to keep in freezer. The color of the strawberries will fade after a few months otherwise; however, if kept in freezer, they will still have a beautiful color, delicious flavor and strawberry perfume after a year's keeping.

Montmorency Cherry Preserves

cooking time about 9 min after
  bringing cherries to boil

utensils
  large heavy kettle
  heatproof bowl
  large metal spoon
  wooden spoon
  1-cup measuring cup
  4-cup or qt measuring cup
  screw-top ½-pt jars

1 cup water
¼ cup lemon juice
4 cups sugar
4 level cups washed, seeded cherries

Wash cherries 3 times. Remove seeds.

Bring water, lemon juice and sugar to rolling boil on
  high heat, stirring now and then so it does not
  stick or burn. Add seeded cherries, bring back to
  rolling boil. Boil 9 min. Remove from heat; test
  by putting a spoonful juice in refrigerator for a
  min. Hold up, if a skin forms on top, it is ready.
  Otherwise, cook and test at 1-min intervals until
  skin forms when tested.

Remove from heat, pour into bowl, remove scum, let
  cool until perfectly cold before ladling into screw-
  top ½-pt jars. Label, keep in freezer for best taste
  and color.

*Here is a trick for more flavor when seeding the cherries—seed them
over a strainer, dropping seeds in strainer and letting juice strain
into bowl. You get about ¼ cup juice, which you substitute for an
equal amount of water. Be careful not to crush or tear cherries when
seeding them. These cherries are a beautiful bright red and have a
real cherry flavor.*

Old-fashioned
Damson Plum Preserves

cooking time about 20 min
after bringing plums
to boil

utensils
wooden spoon
large heavy kettle
qt heatproof measuring
cup
large mixing bowl
metal spoon
small screw-top freezer
jars, ½ pt
makes 5 jars

4 heaping cups washed, seeded, halved
damsons
4 level cups sugar
2 cups water
¼ cup fresh or frozen lemon juice

In kettle on high heat make syrup of sugar and water, stirring now and then so it does not stick or burn. Boil 2-3 min. Add plums to syrup while stirring with wooden spoon. Bring back to boil on high heat. Don't let preserves boil over, as it's very messy to clean the stove. If necessary, reduce heat to medium high. Boil rapidly about 20 min and start testing by taking kettle off heat and putting spoon of juice in saucer to see if skin has formed. If you cannot see skin, replace kettle on high heat and cook 1 min more and test. Do this at minute intervals until skin forms. Then remove from heat; pour carefully (don't splash, as you might get burned) into large heatproof bowl. Remove scum by pushing it toward middle and scooping it up with metal spoon. To remove hard-to-get scum, tear small pieces off a paper towel and float scum off—the paper towel will absorb it. You can only do this while preserves are hot.

Let preserves cool without moving; when cold, spoon into small screw-top jelly jars.

The best place for keeping flavor and color of preserves is your freezer. Here they will keep 2 years without loss of either.

31

Yellow, Green or Purple Plum Preserves

cooking time about 10 min after bringing plums to boil

utensils
wooden spoon
large heavy kettle
qt heatproof measuring cup
large mixing bowl
metal spoon
small screw-top freezer jars, ½ pt
makes 4-5 jars

4 heaping cups, washed, seeded, halved plums
4 level cups sugar
1 cup water
¼ cup lemon juice

In kettle on high heat make syrup of sugar, water and lemon juice and boil 2-3 min, stirring now and then so it does not stick or burn. Add plums to syrup while stirring with wooden spoon. Bring back to boil on high heat. Don't let the preserves boil over, as it's very messy to clean the stove. If necessary, reduce heat to medium high and boil rapidly about 10 min; then start testing by taking kettle off heat and putting a spoon of juice into a saucer in the refrigerator for a few min; then tilting saucer to see if skin has formed. If you cannot see skin, replace kettle on high heat, cook 1 min more and test. Do this at minute intervals until skin forms. Then remove carefully (don't splash as you might get burned), and pour into large heatproof bowl. Remove scum with metal spoon by pushing it toward middle and scooping it up. To remove hard-to-get scum, tear small pieces off a paper towel and float it off. The paper towels will absorb the scum. You can only do this while the preserves are hot.

Let preserves cool without moving; when cold, spoon into small screw-top jelly jars.

The best place to keep the flavor and color of preserves is your freezer. Here they will keep 2 years without loss of either.

32

Black Raspberry Preserves

cooking time about 10 min after
bringing berries to boil

utensils
wooden spoon
large heavy kettle
qt heatproof measuring
cup
large mixing bowl
metal spoon
small screw-top freezer
jars, ½ pt
makes 5-6 jars

1 heaping quart cup washed black raspberries
4 level cups sugar
2 cups water
¼ cup fresh or frozen lemon juice

Make syrup of water, sugar and lemon juice by bringing
to rolling boil on high heat, stirring once in a while
so it doesn't stick or burn. Add raspberries and
bring back to boil. Boil on high heat or medium
high heat 10 min, stirring once in a while and
watching that it doesn't run over. What a mess
to clean up if it does!

Remove from heat. Test by putting teaspoon juice in
saucer and placing in refrigerator 2-3 min, then
tilting it to see if skin has formed. If it hasn't,
place back on heat, cook fast 1 min and test. Continue until it forms skin.

Remove from heat, pour into large heatproof bowl to
cool, and remove scum from top while hot by
moving it with metal spoon to center, then scooping it up. After removing as much as you can, tear
paper towel into small pieces and float on top;
the scum will cling to the paper.

Let preserves stand until cold before removing; then
spoon into the screw-top jars and freeze for best
flavor.

delicious!

Quiche Lorraine

baking time about 8 min for crust, about 25 min for custard
preheat oven 425° for crust, 375° for quiche

utensils
rotary beater
glass pie plate
mixing bowl
saucepan

* "Rosa's Old-fashioned Piecrust" (1 crust) (see its recipe)
8 strips bacon broiled, broken into 1-inch pieces
3 large eggs
1½ cups light cream
½ tsp salt
sprinkle of nutmeg

With sharp prongs of fork punch holes all over bottom and sides of piecrust in pie plate, so it will not balloon up when baking; do not tear crust as you punch holes.

Bake crust in preheated 425° oven, 8 min. Remove from oven, push broiled bacon pieces into crust. Set aside to cool, while you make the custard.

Beat eggs with rotary beater, bring cream to boil, gradually stir cream into eggs, add salt, mix with rotary beater a second before pouring cream mixture into cold baked shell. Sprinkle with nutmeg, place in middle of preheated 375° oven, bake 25 min. Serve from oven to table, can't wait.

Chopped Liver

cooking time 15 min or more

utensils
skillet
meat grinder
mixing bowl
serves about 6

1 lb fresh chicken livers
2 medium-sized onions, sliced
2 hard-boiled eggs
½ cup chicken fat as needed
salt to taste

Sauté the onions in some of the chicken fat until soft but not browned, remove to plate to cool. Sauté the livers until blood doesn't show. Don't burn, don't cook livers dry; juicy livers taste better. Remove to plate to cool.

Grind the livers, onions and hard-boiled eggs together into a bowl. Do not discard any fat on the plates. Add to the ground livers. For a pâté, grind twice. Mix together thoroughly, add salt to taste. If necessary, add a little more melted fat.

You can use vegetable shortening for a different taste.

This chopped liver is good served with crisp radishes and a slice of tomato for lunch or it makes a good hors d'oeuvre. It can be shaped into small balls and dipped in sieved hard-boiled egg yolks to look pretty for a cocktail party. Rye or black bread goes well with chopped liver.

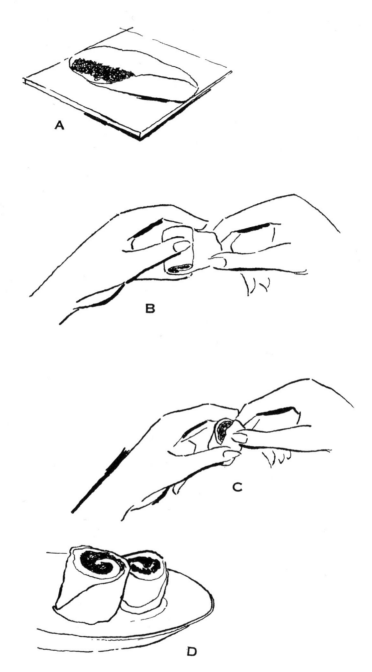

MAKING A BEEF KNISH: (A) meat filling on sheet of dough being rolled (B) unrolling outside layer to form bottom of knish (C) finishing the bottom (D) the knish ready to bake.

Beef Knishes

cooking time about 20 min
preheat oven 375°

utensils
   meat grinder
   rolling pin
   baking sheet
makes about 26

* "Never-fail Double Piecrust" (see its recipe)
2 cups leftover meat loaf, stew, pot roast or any tasty cooked beef ground in meat grinder, seasoning corrected by adding salt and pepper to taste
⅓-½ cup unsweetened mayonnaise to hold ground beef together
For beef without much flavor, seasonings ground and added as suggested in "Party Meat Rolls" (see its recipe)

Divide dough in 4 pieces, roll each into sheet about ⅛ inch thick, 10 inches long, 7 inches wide, one at a time. Spoon the beef mixture across the end of each sheet facing the cook about 2 inches wide. Roll each sheet up lengthwise. Cut into 1-inch pieces. Unroll enough of the outside layer to turn and form the bottom of the knish. See illustration. Repeat until all are made.

You can bake these immediately or you can place in deep freeze on waxed paper. When frozen place in plastic bags until needed. Do not defrost before baking. Bake in preheated oven about 17 min, or if frozen, about 30 min. Serve hot.

Bess' Liver Pâté

cooking time 15-20 min

utensils
  heavy skillet
  meat grinder
  mixing bowl
  small bowl
  electric mixer (optional)
serves 2-3

8 chicken livers or 3 slices calves' liver
1 medium onion, sliced, to fry with liver
¼ small onion, raw
¼ cup vegetable shortening
1 hard-boiled egg
4 Ritz crackers
1 tbsp unsweetened mayonnaise
salt to taste

Fry liver and onion in vegetable shortening, being careful not to burn. Let cool. Grind all ingredients except mayonnaise and salt twice; add remaining vegetable shortening from skillet. Add mayonnaise; put in electric mixer to get smooth or mix by hand. Add salt to taste. Place in small bowl in refrigerator to cool.

When chilled, unmold on plate with parsley and nest of little red radishes.

fix ahead; freezes well

Cocktail Franks in Jackets

baking time about 10 min
  preheat oven 450°

utensils
  board
  rolling pin
  baking sheet
makes about 20 franks

* Never-fail Single Piecrust (see its recipe)
1 (8-oz) can cocktail franks (franks should be 1-1½ inches long; if longer, cut in half)

Roll out dough, cut into 1½-inch squares, place franks on squares, roll dough over franks to close but leave ends open. Bake 10 min on baking sheet. Serve hot.

You can freeze cocktail franks unbaked, freezing on waxed paper and storing in plastic bags. Bake while frozen.

good hors d'oeuvre

Mushroom Appetizer

cooking time 25 min
  preheat oven 325°

utensils
  pyrex dish to fit mush-
    rooms
  foil to cover
serves 4

12 large (not huge) mushrooms, stems removed and minced
melted butter to dip mushrooms
3 tbsp parsley, minced fine
3 tbsp white bulb of scallions or onions,
  minced fine
juice of ½ lemon
1 tsp melted butter to mix with minced
  vegetables
salt to taste
pepper to taste
6 tsp heavy cream to mix with minced
  vegetables
6 tsp heavy cream to top mushrooms

Wipe mushrooms dry. Dip in melted butter. Combine
the minced mushroom stems, scallions, parsley,
lemon juice, melted butter, salt and pepper to taste
and 6 tsp cream. Spoon into the mushrooms, top
each one with ½ tsp cream.

Arrange in baking dish, cover with foil, bake 25 min.

These are just as good to eat as they look.

~6 qts~

~4 qts~

~2 qts~

HANDY KETTLE. Can be used to make soups, steam seafood, boil matzo balls, boil
"Rice—The French Method" (see its recipe), cook preserves, cook spaghetti.

fix ahead; freezes well

Mama's Chicken Noodle Soup

cooking time 1 hr, 15 min

utensils
    saucepan without lid
    strainer
makes 5-6 cups

3-3½ lb fryer with giblets, washed under cold running water
5-6 cups cold tap water
1 small onion, peeled
1 stalk celery, washed
1 carrot, peeled
1 small parsnip, peeled
salt to taste
1½ cups thin noodles

Bring water, chicken, onion, celery, carrot, parsnip to a boil, reduce to low, simmer about 1 hr 15 min. Add salt to taste. The chicken should be tender but not fall apart.

Remove chicken from broth, strain broth, put in refrigerator to congeal fat, lift off fat.

Cook noodles according to directions on package. Heat broth, add noodles, correct seasoning, cook gently 1 min. The broth should be rich and tasty.

You can take the chicken off the bones, add to the noodles and broth for a meal in a dish. Or you can slice the cold chicken for sandwiches, salad or make chicken pies and chicken à la king.

An added bonus is to make more chicken broth as follows: save the chicken bones and skin, cover with cold water, add aromatic seasonings, carrot, onion, celery, parsnip, simmer 2½-3 hr, season and strain.

fix ahead; freezes well

Pennsylvania Dutch Chicken Corn Soup

cooking time 1 hr, 15 min or more

utensils
large saucepan
serves 7-8

3-3½ lb fryer with giblets, washed under running water
5-6 cups tap water
1 carrot
1 onion
1 parsnip
1 stalk celery
1¼ cups fresh, frozen or canned corn
2 cups medium-sized noodles, cooked as per directions on pkg
* 3 "Tender Hard-boiled Eggs" (see its recipe)
salt to taste
grind of pepper

Bring chicken, cold water and vegetables except corn to boil, reduce heat, simmer about 1 hr 15 min, adding salt to taste. Chicken should be tender but not fall apart. Remove chicken.

Strain soup, put in refrigerator to congeal fat, lift off fat.

Remove chicken from bones, save skin and bones to use later. Cut chicken in large pieces, return to broth on medium heat, add corn, noodles, slice eggs and add last. Correct seasoning. Bring soup to boil, add grind of pepper to taste. Serve soup very hot.

Make broth to use later from cooked chicken bones and skin, proceeding as in "Mama's Chicken Noodle Soup" (see its recipe) to have extra broth on hand, a bonus.

41

European Matzo Balls in Rich Chicken Broth

cooking time 30 min after bringing to boil

utensils
electric mixer or rotary beater
mixing bowl
large kettle
large saucepan
serves 5 or 6

* Broth from "Mama's Chicken Noodle Soup" (see its recipe)
20 cups tap water
2 tsp salt

MATZO BALLS

3 eggs, whites separated from yolks, yolks broken up with fork
¾ cup matzo meal
¼ tsp salt
2 tbsp melted chicken fat or vegetable shortening, cooled
¼ cup chicken broth, cooled

Whip egg whites stiff in small bowl of mixer at high speed or use wire whip or rotary beater. Gradually fold in yolks; then gradually fold in matzo meal, salt and fat; last the broth. Place in refrigerator 30 min.

In large kettle, bring about 20 cups water to boil with 2 tsp salt. With 2 iced tea spoons shape and push a spoonful matzo ball mixture into boiling water. Work as fast as you can. Continue until all have been dropped in. Put lid on kettle, reduce heat to medium high, boil gently 30 min without looking or lifting lid.

Bring chicken broth to boil, remove matzo balls from boiling water with slotted spoon, drop into the hot chicken broth and serve.

Matzo balls can be kept 3 months or longer when frozen in chicken broth, with no loss of flavor.

fix ahead; freezes well
In Chinese, "Won Ton Soup"; In America, "Delicious"

Kreplach Soup

cooking time kreplach about 25 min; chicken soup made earlier

utensils
kettle with lid
pastry board
rolling pin
grater
skillet
mixing bowl
makes 160 small kreplachs

FILLING

2 cups stewed, potted, or cooked leftover beef ground once
1 stalk celery, strings scraped off
1 small onion (about ¼ cup)
2 tsp margarine
2 small eggs, broken up with fork
pinch cinnamon
1 tsp salt to taste
pepper to taste
Soften onion in margarine on low heat; don't brown. Cool. Grate celery over ground beef and add rest of ingredients, mixing with your hand or a spoon. Set aside while you make the dough.
Put large kettle of water with 1 tbsp salt to boil in meantime.

ALTERNATE FILLING

2 cups cooked, potted or stewed, beef ground once
½ tsp celery powder
1 tsp onion powder
2 small eggs, broken up with fork
pinch cinnamon
1 tsp salt to taste
pepper to taste
Combine all ingredients, set aside while you make dough. Put large kettle of water with 1 tbsp salt to boil in meantime.

KREPLACH DOUGH

2 cups flour
2 extra large eggs
¼ tsp salt
⅓ cup water

Sprinkle salt over flour and make a well to put in the eggs, work flour into eggs, adding water as needed. Make a ball, put on pastry board, sprinkle with a little flour and knead dough ball about 5-6 min until it is smooth. Divide in half, roll each half out from center into a thin circle, 15 inches in diameter. Be sure to lift as you roll so dough will not stick. Lift just before cutting each half in squares to be sure they do not stick. With sharp knife cut into squares.

Put a little filling on each square, fold like a triangle. Pinch shut so it doesn't open. Continue until all squares have been filled and folded.

Drop kreplach, one at a time into the boiling water, boil 25 min with a lid. Remove kreplach with slotted spoon, drop into rich homemade chicken broth. Serve at once or freeze. These freeze beautifully, especially in chicken broth.

43

fix ahead; freezes well

Homemade Vegetable Soup

cooking time about 3½ hr

utensils
soup kettle with lid
serves 9-10

3 lb meaty short ribs of beef, chuck, shin bone or brisket
beef or chicken bones
10 cups cold tap water
2 carrots, peeled
1 large onion
1 stalk celery and leaves
1 turnip, peeled
1 no. 303 can stewed tomatoes (about 2 cups)
¼ cup each lima beans, diced carrots, string beans, peas, diced celery, corn
½ cup shredded cabbage or 2 leaves Boston lettuce
1 tsp salt or more to taste
pepper to taste

Bring the water, beef and bones, carrots, onion, turnip and celery to boil. Partially cover with lid, reduce to simmer, simmer 3 hr, remove onion, celery, carrots, turnip and bones.

Add stewed tomatoes, lima beans; cook 10 min. Then add diced carrots, string beans, peas; cook 10 min, add salt to taste. Now add diced celery, corn, shredded cabbage or lettuce, cook 10 more min, correct seasoning, and add grind of pepper to taste.

This soup may be eaten at once but tastes better if left to season in refrigerator overnight. If you have used short ribs, chuck or brisket, serve them with a little of the hot broth over them and some red horseradish seasoned with pinch of sugar.

Lima Bean Soup

cooking time 3 hr

utensils
    large saucepan with lid
makes about 10 cups

2½-3 lb short ribs of beef, cut into pieces,
    or other good soup meat
10 cups cold water
1½ cups dried baby lima beans
1 cup large dried lima beans
¼ cup medium barley, washed in strainer
    under running water
2 large onions, peeled
3 carrots, peeled
2 stalks celery with leaves, washed
salt to taste
grind of pepper to taste

Bring water, beef, vegetables, beans and barley to boil.
Reduce to simmer, put lid on, simmer 3 hr, stir
once in a while to keep from sticking.

Add salt to taste after it is midway in cooking. Remove
beef, carrots, onions, celery and spoon off as much
fat as possible. Correct seasoning, add grind of
pepper, serve very hot.

*The beef can be eaten "as is" in the hot soup or just as a meat course
with horseradish on the side and Polish-style pickles.*

what it says, "a quickie"

Quickie Bean Soup

cooking time 10 min

utensils
    saucepan
makes 4 cups

1 no. 202 can or 2 cups Cannelli, marrow
    or Great Northern beans
2 cups canned chicken broth
1 8-oz can stewed tomatoes
½ carrot, shredded
pepper to taste

Stir chicken broth into beans, add rest of ingredients.
Bring to boil, reduce heat to low, cook 10 min
to blend flavors, add pepper to taste.

like grandma used to make—fix ahead; freezes fine

Rich Thick Lentil Soup

cooking time 3 hr

utensils
    strainer
    large saucepan with lid
    metal spoon
    slotted spoon
makes about 10 cups

2½-3 lb short ribs of beef or other soup meat, washed quickly under running water
10 cups tap water
2 large onions, peeled
2 carrots, peeled
2 stalks celery and leaves, washed
1 Idaho potato, peeled and cut in quarters
2 cups lentils, washed in strainer under running water
salt to taste
grind of pepper
5 kosher-style frankfurters, ½ frank per person

Bring water, beef, fresh vegetables to boil, reduce heat, simmer about 2 hr, add salt to taste.

If you wish to remove the fat, strain out beef and vegetables; set aside while you place broth in refrigerator to congeal fat. Lift off fat.

Bring soup back to boil, put in beef and vegetables, add lentils, simmer about 1 hr, add salt as needed. With slotted spoon lift onion, celery, carrot, some potatoes and a cup or so lentils and mash with metal spoon through strainer back into soup to thicken and flavor it.

Slice frankfurters, add, bring back to boil, boil 5 min, gently. Serve very hot.

What could be more delicious on a cold winter's night than this lentil soup with thick slices of fresh pumpernickel? Even in summer when we are tired of cold soups and cold salads, there are requests for lentil soup.

46

Green or Yellow Split Pea Soup

cooking time 3 hr

utensils
strainer
large saucepot with lid
slotted spoon
makes 10-12 cups

2½ lb meaty short ribs or other soup meat, washed quickly under running water
10 cups cold tap water
1 large onion, peeled
2 carrots, peeled
1 stalk celery and leaves, washed
1-lb pkg split peas, washed in strainer under running water
salt and pepper to taste

Bring the water, beef, fresh vegetables to boil. Put lid on. Simmer for 1½ hr, add salt lightly. Strain beef and vegetables, set aside while you place soup in the refrigerator to congeal fat. Lift off fat.

Bring broth, beef, vegetables to a boil, add split peas, bring back to boil, reduce to simmer for 1½ hr, correct seasoning.

With slotted spoon remove onions, celery, carrots to wire strainer over soup, mash with metal spoon, back into soup. This adds flavor. Correct seasoning, add pepper, remove beef, serve soup hot.

Split pea, like most soups, keeps well in the refrigerator for a couple of days. Flavored "croutettes" are delicious sprinkled over the soup just before eating, so they will be crisp.

Quickie Pea Soup

cooking time 5 min

utensils
saucepan
makes about 6 cups

4 cups canned chicken broth
2 cups canned green pea soup
sprinkle of fresh-ground pepper

Stir chicken broth into pea soup, bring to boil. Stir, boil 2 min, serve boiling hot with a grind of pepper and some "croutettes" sprinkled at the table to ensure crispness.

good enough for a dinner party—fix ahead; a quickie

Minute-made Petite Marmite Soup

cooking time about 15 min

utensils
  saucepan
  steamer
serves 12

3 boxes (2 pkgs to box), Knorr's spring vegetable soup
10 cups water
½ cup carrots, cut long into ½-inch matchsticks
½ cup celery, cut as above
½ cup turnips, cut as above
½ cup scallions, the little white bulb cut into thin circles and the green part cut long into ½-inch matchsticks

Bring the soup and water to a boil, reduce heat, cook 10 minutes, strain.

Steam vegetables (see "Steaming") about 3 min, taste for doneness, don't overcook; or boil them in water to cover just until done, remove immediately from heat, run cold water over them to stop the cooking, put into broth, heat, serve piping hot.

You can pass some grated parmesan cheese for those who like it.

a quickie

Jiffy Different Pea Soup

cooking time about 5 min

utensils
  saucepan
serves 4

1 can Campbell's pea soup
1 can tomato soup
1 cup water, or Knorr's spring vegetable soup, strained, or Knorr's chicken noodle soup, strained
pepper to taste

Off heat stir pea soup and tomato soup together, then stir in the water or preferred soup. Heat about 5 min, correct the seasoning and the soup is ready.

for a summer day—a quickie; no cooking

Cold Vegetable Soup

utensils
  electric blender
serves 5-6

2 cans (11-oz) vegetable soup
½ cup chicken broth, canned
4 tbsp sour cream
½ tsp dried dill
¼ tsp celery seed, ground fine
pepper to taste
½ cup finely minced scallions
2 tbsp sour cream to garnish soup

Place all ingredients in blender except scallion and the 2 tbsp sour cream, flipping off and on, on high speed for 10 seconds until everything is blended smooth.

Place in refrigerator until needed. Serve in glass bowls, float sour cream on top with sprinkle of scallion and serve cold.

You can vary this recipe by substituting another kind of canned vegetable soup.

49

a quickie for a hot day; fix ahead—"Look Ma, no cooking!"

Cold Vegetable Creamed Soup

utensils
blender
wire strainer
serves 4

1 can vegetable bean soup
½ cup chicken broth
2 tbsp sour cream
pepper to taste
1 hard-boiled egg yolk pushed through strainer
2 tbsp finely chopped parsley
4 tbsp sour cream to float on top of soup

Blend all ingredients together except parsley and the 4 tbsp sour cream, turning off and on about 10 times on high speed.

Place in refrigerator to get cold. Serve in individual glass bowls, float 1 tbsp sour cream on top and decorate with minced parsley.

Potted Chuck Roast

cooking time 2½-3 hr
   preheat oven 400°

utensils
   casserole with lid
   skillet
serves 6

3½-lb chuck roast or chuck in 1 piece, room temperature
2 tbsp fat or more if needed
3 cups canned onion broth, strained, or dehydrated onion soup prepared as directed on pkg
1 cup water
½ cup ketchup
4 carrots, sliced in 1-inch pieces
¼ cup celery, diced
2 bay leaves
2 allspice
4 tbsp flour
1 tsp salt to taste
grind of pepper to taste

Wipe roast dry with paper towels before browning in fat in skillet. Remove to casserole. Remove fat from skillet; add onion broth, water, ketchup, stirring in the good brownings and add carrots, celery, bay leaves and set aside.

Sprinkle 2 tbsp flour on roast before placing in oven 5 min. Do the same to other side, shaking to spread flour.

Bring onion mixture to boil, pour over roast, sprinkle salt on, place in oven. When it bubbles, put lid on, reduce heat to 300°, baste now and then, roast 1½ hr before turning over; continue roasting and basting until tender about 1 or more hrs. Grind a little pepper on to taste.

Place roast sauce in refrigerator for fat to harden before removing. Remove fat. Slice roast, heat in sauce. Broad noodles go well with this roast.

Rump Roast with Wine and Sauce

cooking time 3-3½ hr

utensils
    casserole with lid
    rack
serves 8

4-5 lb rump or chuck roast in 1 piece, room temperature
1 large onion, chopped fine
4 tbsp fat
2 tbsp flour
1 cup hot water
1 cup tomato sauce
½ cup sherry wine
3 tsp sugar
1 tsp Accent
1 tsp salt
pepper to taste

Soften onion in some of the fat, remove to plate. Wipe roast, flour it, brown it in remaining fat, remove to plate, then remove any fat but leave brownings in casserole.

Make sauce by adding hot water, tomato sauce, sherry wine and sugar to brownings, scraping them up for flavor before putting in rack and placing roast on it. Sprinkle salt, Accent and onions on roast, turn heat to high until sauce bubbles, reduce heat to simmer, put lid on. Simmer 3-3½ hr, basting often.

The gimmick in this roast is keeping the roast out of the sauce, yet getting the delicious flavor by basting with the sauce. If you have any left over, don't worry; it's delicious served cold as well as made into other dishes.

Fruited Chuck Roast

cooking time 3-3½ hr
preheat oven 325°

utensils
close-fitting bowl
heavy casserole with lid
saucepan
serves 6-8

3½-4 lb chuck roast in one piece or sirloin tip roast in one piece
2½ cups canned pineapple juice
1½ cups canned grapefruit juice
½ cup dry sherry or burgundy wine
1 large onion, peeled and sliced
2 bay leaves
2 allspice
2 tbsp or more margarine, half butter, half vegetable shortening or oil

Marinate beef in close-fitting bowl in liquid and seasonings 2-4 hr, turning once or twice.

Wipe beef dry, set marinade aside, then brown beef on medium heat, turning frequently.

Pour half the heated marinade over the beef, cover, roast about 2½ hr, adding more heated marinade as needed.

Roast another half hour, uncovered, being sure there is enough delicious sauce to serve.

Flavor Savor Pot Roast

cooking time 2-2½ hr

utensils
    casserole with lid
    skillet
serves 4-5

2½-3 lb chuck in 1 piece, room temperature
2 tbsp flour
4 large onions, minced
4 tbsp fat as needed
1 tsp salt
1 bottle chili sauce
pepper to taste

Over medium heat brown flour a beige color, stirring all the while; don't burn. Set aside, wipe skillet if necessary, sauté onions soft; set aside while browning chuck well (takes about 20 min), rub on salt, flour before placing it in casserole with onions.

Pour hot chili sauce over roast before covering, turn heat to low, simmer 2-2½ hr, being careful not to burn, baste once in a while.

This roast has a delicious winey taste.

easy to make to enjoy your guests and for your guests to enjoy—fix ahead; freezes well

Chuck Roast
in Mushroom Sauce

cooking time 2½ hr

utensils
    casserole with lid
serves 4-5

2½ lb chuck in one piece, room temperature
2 tbsp fat
1 can (10½-oz) cream of mushroom soup
1 can (12½-oz) onion soup, strained
                            or
1 pkg dehydrated onion soup (Knorr's) as per instructions on pkg, using 2 cups water, strained before using
4 tbsp sherry
salt and pepper to taste
butter balls made of 1 tbsp butter mixed with 1 tbsp flour

Brown chuck well in casserole over medium heat; then set aside while you remove fat but leave brownings; gradually stir in mushroom soup, scraping up brownings, gradually stir in onion soup and sherry, bring to boil before adding chuck. Reduce heat to low, put lid on, simmer about 2½ hr until tender. Correct seasoning, add pepper.

If sauce is thin, gradually drop tiny butter balls to thicken it (see "Thickenings—How Much and How?").

This dish reheats and freezes beautifully.

doesn't have to be watched

Rich Man's Rib Roast

cooking time 16 min/lb for rare, 18 min for medium rare, plus 15 min out of the oven
preheat oven 400°

utensils
shallow roaster pan

a 3-rib roast, well marbled—fat running through it, not just on the outside; with a bright red, fresh look

Put it in for the minutes needed.

Let the roast rest on its bones 15 min outside the oven after it is roasted. It will then be juicer and easier to slice.

The top will be crusty brown, the inside will be deliciously tender. Two outside slices will be well done; remaining slices will be rare and juicy.

Dip juice gently over beef when serving. A sprinkle of salt, a grind of pepper, and you have a meal that will be remembered.

Getting the right cut insures your special night. Ask for first cut. For tenderness, be sure it shows fat all over. Do not accept beef that is dark and dried out; it could have been packaged for several days. If the butcher cuts the roast with longer ribs than you like, ask him to cut the ribs off short and cut them in pieces for making soup or braising.

doesn't have to be watched

Thrifty Rib Roast

cooking time	min/lb	meat thermometer	
rare	18-20	140°	3 standing ribs, first cut
medium rare	20-25	145°	salt to taste
medium	25-30	155°-160°	
well done	30-35	165°-170°	

3 ribs, 8-lb weight, takes about 2½ hr for rare.
4 ribs, 12-lb weight, takes about 3½ hr for rare.
preheat oven 325°

utensils
   shallow roaster
serves 6

Roast ribs on their bones according to the table at 325°.
Salt roast lightly midway in roasting.

When roasted, let rest 15-30 min to make carving easier.

This is the thrifty way to get less shrinkage, more roast for your money and more money to spend on the "trimmings" for your "dining out at home."

a quickie; fix ahead

Hamburgers
à la Sherry

cooking time 8-10 min

utensils
   mixing bowl
   skillet
serves 2-3

1 lb ground beef
2 tbsp grated onion
2 tbsp dry sherry
½ tsp salt to taste
pepper to taste
butter or margarine to fry

Mix all ingredients lightly, shape into ovals. Heat the skillet hot with a little fat, before browning hamburgers on both sides. Reduce heat to low, sauté them as you prefer about 2 or more min on each side.

Serve on heated plate.

Tenderloin Deluxe

baking time 30-35 min
    preheat oven 450°

utensils
    shallow roasting pan with
      rack
serves 6-8

4-6 lb tenderloin, in one piece, uniform thickness (if necessary tie ends to be same thickness or cut off ends to have tenderloin one thickness)
butter to smear on tenderloin and melted butter to baste

Place the tenderloin smeared with softened butter on rack in middle of oven, and roast 30-35 min. Baste once.

The roast will be brown on the outside and juicy rare on the inside. Be sure to serve on heated plates.

This is a wonderful dish for special guests but be sure that the guests are in the house before baking. To bard the tenderloin means to tie small strips of fat around the tenderloin. Rubbing softened butter over the tenderloin is just as good. However, with our quality beef in the U. S. A., we don't need to do this. Be sure to tell your sophisticated friends they can skip this extra chore.

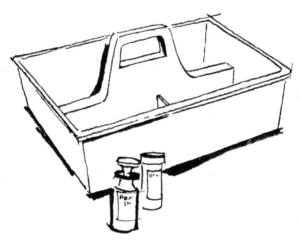

SPICE AND HERB CARRIER. This is a wonderful way to keep your spices and herbs together. You can carry it easily, wherever you want to work with it. You can store it easily; it is quiet and keeps the spices and herbs available when and where you want them. It is inexpensive and can be bought at 5 & 10¢ stores.

fix ahead; delicious hot or cold

Party Brisket

cooking time 3½ hr

utensils
    large casserole with lid
serves 8-10

1 whole brisket, 7-8 lb
4 tbsp fat
2 cups chili sauce
4 large onions, sliced thin
about 1½ tsp salt
pepper to taste
½ tsp garlic salt
paprika
3 bay leaves
4 allspice
3 tbsp light brown sugar, not the "brown-ulated" kind

Brown brisket on medium heat, remove to plate, throw fat away but swish chili sauce into the good brownings before replacing brisket and adding rest of ingredients except sugar and half the salt.

Roast in oven 2 hr with lid on, basting now and then.

Add ¾ tsp salt, continue to roast 1½ hr, test for tenderness; don't overcook as it will be stringy.

Sprinkle 3 tbsp brown sugar over brisket and glaze in broiler on lowest shelf, being most careful not to burn.

Strain sauce, remove fat by congealing in the refrigerator.

When ready to serve, slice the delicious brisket; heat in sauce without a lid.

Beef Stew for Men

cooking time 2-2½ hr
  preheat oven 450°

utensils
  rubber spatula
  skillet
  casserole with lid
serves 8

4-lb chuck roast, 2-inch pieces, room temperature
8 carrots each cut into 3 pieces
1 tbsp fat to glaze carrots
1½ tbsp sugar
4 tbsp fat as needed
4 tbsp flour
3 cups strained, canned onion soup, or dehydrated onion soup as per instructions, or 4 onion bouillon cubes diluted in 3 cups water
1 cup red burgundy wine
3 tbsp tomato sauce
4 allspice
2 large bay leaves
1 tsp thyme
3 large garlic cloves
¼ tsp pepper to taste
1½ tsp salt or more to taste

Glaze carrots by melting fat, adding sugar over carrots, shaking, rolling them around until glazed; then set aside on plate, getting all the glaze up with a rubber spatula.

Wash out skillet, heat with 1 tbsp fat, brown beef, adding fat as needed; avoid crowding, so as to brown better. Place in casserole; remove fat from skillet but leave brownings in; set aside while you sprinkle 2 tbsp flour over beef in casserole, shake to distribute it, heat in oven 5 min, sprinkle other 2 tbsp flour and shake, heat 5 min.

Pour rest of ingredients into skillet, scraping up brownings, and bring to boil. Pour over beef in casserole, adding carrots, bring back to boil before putting in the oven with lid on. Reduce heat to 300°. Cook, stirring once in a while, 2-2½ hr. Correct seasoning.

60

Party Goulash

cooking time 2½-3 hr

utensils
  skillet
  casserole with lid
serves 8

4 lb beef, chuck preferred, cut into bite-size pieces, room temperature
1½ cups diced onion or frozen minced onions
8 tbsp fat
3 tsp paprika
1½ cups orange juice
1 tsp salt to taste
2 tsp marjoram
1 cup white wine or sauterne
1 cup sour cream, room temperature (optional)

Sauté onion in skillet in tbsp fat until golden color. Place in casserole.

On high heat brown beef in little fat as needed. Beef will curl; don't crowd, set aside.

Sprinkle onion with paprika, stir on high heat 1 min. before adding orange juice, salt, marjoram, beef. Bring to boil, reduce to simmer, put lid on, simmer 2 hr, stirring occasionally.

Add wine to goulash, bring to boil, reduce heat, simmer without lid 30 min to thicken.

Off heat stir a little goulash sauce into sour cream to heat it. Slowly stir back into goulash; heat, don't boil. Sour cream will curdle.

Broad noodles are fine with goulash. If you plan to freeze goulash, don't add sour cream until you use it. This goulash is also delicious without sour cream.

a quickie: freezes well

Beef Stroganoff

cooking time about 30 min

utensils
    skillet
    saucepan

serves **4**

2-lb tenderloin, strip or porterhouse steak, cut into 2-inch long strips by ¼-inch thick, at room temperature
3 tbsp butter
4 tbsp flour
3 cups strained onion soup or dehydrated onion soup as per instructions on pkg, or onion bouillon cubes diluted in 1½ cups water
1 tbsp and 1 tsp A-1 sauce
1 tbsp Worcestershire sauce
3 tbsp fat
½ lb mushrooms, sliced or 1 cup canned mushrooms
½ cup sour cream, room temperature
salt and pepper to taste

Melt butter. Off heat stir in flour, gradually add all but ½ cup onion soup. Stir, cook on medium heat until thickened and smooth before adding A-1 sauce and Worcestershire sauce, then set aside. This can be done earlier.

Brown mushrooms in skillet on high, stirring, shaking to keep mushrooms from burning, but brown lightly before removing to plate. This can be done earlier.

Add tsp fat or more as needed to brown beef strips quickly. Don't crowd as steaks will steam, not brown. Move skillet off and on high heat to brown quickly. Set aside on a plate. Add the ½ cup onion soup which was set aside, scraping up brownings for flavor before adding sauce, steak strips, mushrooms and salt to taste.

Off heat, gradually stir a little of the hot sauce into sour cream until about ½ cup has been added, then stir back into the sauce. Heat but do not boil, as sour cream may curdle.

Grind pepper to taste over the beef Stroganoff.

Serve at once with "Steamed Rice" (see its recipe) on one side and steamed carrots (see "Steaming" and "Tested Times for Steaming Vegetables") on the other.

A nice touch is added by steaming tiny black currants (see "Steaming") 3 min and stirring them with 2 forks into the rice to keep it fluffy.

Swiss Steak Bliss

cooking time 2-2½ hr

utensils
    large skillet with lid
    2-qt saucepan
    aluminum foil
serves 6

2 lb top round steak, room temperature
2 tbsp flour
½ tsp salt to add to flour
1 tsp fat or more
1½ cups canned onion soup, strained, or dehydrated onion soup made as directed on pkg, or onion broth made with 3 bouillon cubes
½ cup cold water
1 4-oz can sliced mushrooms
1½ tsp Worcestershire sauce
½ cup sauterne
2 allspice
¼ tsp thyme
¼ tsp basil
salt and pepper to taste
* butter balls (see "Thickenings—How Much and How")

Dredge steak with salted flour before browning in skillet, set aside.

Combine all ingredients down to salt and pepper, bring to boil, simmer 2 min, pour over steak, cover with aluminum foil, put lid on, simmer 2-2½ hr until steak is fork-tender.

If sauce is thin, thicken with butter balls by dropping a few at a time while simmering until right consistency.

Riced potatoes go well with this dish.

63

leftovers but glamorous; fix ahead

Shepherd's Pie

cooking time 35 min
preheat oven 400°

utensils
saucepan
individual casseroles
serves 4

4 cups leftover cubed beef
4 cups canned onion soup, strained, or dehydrated onion soup
¼ cup diced celery
¼ cup diced green pepper
2 cloves garlic
1 cup diced Idaho potato
2 allspice
1 small bay leaf
½ cup dry sherry
2 (10-oz) pkg frozen minced vegetables
1 (10-oz) pkg frozen peas
1 (10-oz) pkg frozen string beans
salt and pepper to taste
* butter balls as needed (see "Thickenings
—How Much and How")
1 pkg dehydrated whipped potatoes or 2
large or 3 medium Idaho potatoes,
freshly whipped
1 tbsp butter or margarine to dot whipped
potatoes

To onion soup add all ingredients except beef, butter
balls, whipped potatoes, butter, and salt and pepper.
Bring to a boil; gently boil 10 min before adding
beef, salt and pepper to taste.

Add butter balls, stirring one at a time to thicken as you
like it, on medium heat. This takes a few min.

Place in individual casseroles, top with whipped potatoes, dot with butter.

Bake in oven 20-25 min until golden brown.

64

fix ahead; meat balls freeze well

Saucy Meat Balls

cooking time 15-20 min

utensils
  mixing bowl
  cooky sheet
  saucepan
serves 6-8

MEAT BALLS

2 lb ground beef
½ cup dried onion soup mix
½ cup ketchup
½ cup water
about ½ cup bread crumbs

SAUCE

1 bottle chili sauce
1 (20-oz) glass grape jelly
1 cup water
4 tbsp (¼ cup) sauterne

Mix meat ball ingredients together. Shape into balls size of a quarter. Be sure they are firm enough not to fall apart.

Broil on cooky sheet until lightly browned, set aside while making sauce.

Bring sauce ingredients to boil, stirring constantly; reduce heat, simmer 5 min. Drop in meat balls, simmer 10 min.

To freeze, don't brown meat balls, place on cooky sheet, freeze. When frozen, store in plastic bags. When ready to use, brown without defrosting.

fix ahead; freezes well

Meat Balls
in Brandy Sauce

cooking time 30-45 min

utensils
large mixing bowl
saucepan, no lid
skillet (teflon is fine)
serves 8

MEAT BALLS
4 slices bread, Pepperidge or
    Arnold with crust cut off
1 cup milk
2 lb lean ground beef
1 large onion, peeled
2 slightly mixed eggs
salt to taste
¼ tsp pepper
2 tbsp margarine or butter to
    fry meat balls

BRANDY SAUCE
3 pkg Knorr's dehydrated golden onion
    soup mixed into 9 cups water, pre-
    pared according to instructions on pkg
    and strained
1 (8-oz) can whole mushrooms, strained
    mushrooms set aside, broth added to
    onion soup
3 tbsp Worcestershire sauce
2 tbsp A-1 sauce
½ cup sherry
1 cup brandy
5 tbsp tomato sauce
3 tbsp currant jelly
¼ tsp tabasco
¾ tsp basil steeped in ¼ cup boiling water
    15 min, then strained
½ tsp savory steeped in ¼ cup boiling
    water 15 min, then strained
¼ tsp chives steeped in 2 tbsp boiling water
    15 min, then strained
¼ tsp salt to taste
1 large bay leaf or 2 medium leaves
4 whole allspice
1 whole clove garlic
6 tbsp cornstarch mixed with ¼ cup water

Mix bread and milk together with your fingers until
    thoroughly combined before adding ground beef.

Grate onion over beef, add eggs; then mix with your
    fingers thoroughly, adding salt and pepper to taste.

Shape into balls the size of large marble; don't over-
    handle. Wet your hands in bowl of tap water to
    shape balls easier. Place on tray covered with wax
    paper for convenience when you fry.

Preheat greased skillet until hot, test with one ball before
    frying a skilletfull; to brown better, don't over-

66

crowd. Brown both top and bottom, but don't burn before dropping into simmering sauce. Continue until all are added to sauce, simmer about 25 min, stirring in the cornstarch mixture, and cook about 5 min to thicken and clear sauce. The meat balls will be very tender; the sauce will have a rich tangy taste.

This recipe sounds difficult but it is very simple. You'll love it served with hot rice mixed with heated, strained, canned green grapes.

fix ahead; freezes well

Spaghetti Sauce

cooking time 2½-3 hr

utensils
  large lidless saucepot
serves 16

2 lb ground beef, ground once
¼ cup oil, more or less, to fry
5 cans (no. 2½) tomato puree
1 cup canned onion soup or 1 cup water added to 1 envelope Knorr's dehydrated onion soup
2 (6-oz) cans vegetable juice
½ cup dry sherry
1 tsp sugar to taste
2 bay leaves
4 allspice
4 cloves garlic
½ cup water
salt and pepper to taste

Brown beef in fat, stirring, being careful not to burn. Add rest of ingredients, bring to boil, stirring all the while. Reduce heat to simmer, simmer 2½-3 hr, correct seasoning.

This is not only an excellent sauce for spaghetti but a lasagne sauce too.

Party Meat Rolls

cooking time 18-20 min
  preheat oven 450°

utensils
  skillet
  meat grinder
  baking sheet
makes 4 rolls

* dough for 1-crust "Rosa's Old-fashioned
    Piecrust" (see its recipe)
½ cup minced onion
2 tbsp fat as needed
2 cups ground cooked beef (leftover) or
    meat loaf
½ cup unsweetened mayonnaise
½ tsp salt to taste
¾ tsp ground celery salt
½ tsp nutmeg
¼ tsp cinnamon
½ tsp ground allspice
a good grind of pepper
1 egg yolk mixed with 1 tsp water to glaze
    rolls or softened butter or margarine to
    brush on

Sauté onions until soft, not browned; set aside to cool.

Grind cooked beef with sautéed onions. Mix in rest of
    filling ingredients by hand. Correct seasoning.

Divide dough into 4 portions, roll one at a time into
    10″ x 5″ strip, fill, spreading filling about 1″
    wide, bring the 2 long sides together, fold over,
    glaze with egg yolks and water or softened butter
    or margarine, place on baking sheet. Continue until
    all are made. Bake in oven 18-20 min. These rolls
    may be served hot or cold, but hot is better. Cut
    into bite-size pieces.

*These rolls are delicious served with a cocktail, tomato juice, or hot
soup. To freeze leave in rolls.*

Lasagne

cooking time about 1 hr
preheat oven 350°

utensils
large bowl
grater
saucepan
heatproof baking dish 7"
x 10"

serves 4

1 pkg lasagne or ¼ of 1-lb pkg 2½-inch
square noodles
1 lb ricotta cheese
1 8-oz piece mozzarella cheese
½ cup grated parmesan cheese
1 slice bread, crust removed
¼ cup milk
1 lb ground beef
1 small onion
1 egg
¾ tsp salt to taste
pepper to taste
1 tsp fat or more to fry

SAUCE
3¾ cups canned marinara sauce or 3 (10-oz)
cans sauce
6 tbsp dry sherry
¼ tsp salt to taste

Follow directions on lasagne pkg or square noodle pkg
(sometimes called "Bot Bows"). Keep until needed
in large bowl in cold water to keep from sticking.

Crumble bread and milk together, add ground beef,
grate onion on, add egg, salt, pepper, mix with
hand, shape into 1-inch flat cakes. Brown in fat
lightly. Set aside.

Bring to boil sauce ingredients, reduce heat, cook uncovered 5 min, divide into 3 portions.

Place one portion sauce in baking dish, arrange lasagne
or squares on it, then layer mozzarella, meat balls,
ricotta and repeat until all are used. Top with
sauce, sprinkle on parmesan cheese, bake 45 min
in oven.

Lasagne can be frozen in a metal dish as it can go
from freezer to oven; just add 30 min to cooking
time. Also double the recipe to save work—eat
one, freeze one.

You can vary lasagne by browning ground beef instead
of making cakes, which saves time and is very tasty.

69

fix ahead

Casserole Meat Loaf

cooking time 1½-2 hr
    preheat oven 325°

utensils
    mixing bowl
    grater
    casserole, no lid
    saucepan
serves 6-8

2 lb ground beef
3 slices day-old bread with crust removed
1 cup milk
1 medium onion
2 eggs
1½ tsp salt to taste
good grind of pepper
butter for casserole
½ cup ketchup
1 cup strained, canned onion soup or water

Crumble bread into milk, add ground beef, grate onion on, add eggs, salt, pepper, mix lightly with fingers but don't overmix.

Spoon mixture, loaf-shape, into buttered casserole, do not press.

Make sauce by bringing ketchup and onion soup to boil. Pour half around meat loaf. Bake in oven 1½ hr or more, basting with sauce and adding more as needed.

If there is any leftover meat loaf, make sandwiches or stew by cubing it, combining with strained onion soup, mixed frozen vegetables, diced celery, green pepper, salt and pepper to taste. Heat together 10-15 min before adding butter balls to thicken (see "Thickenings—How Much and How").

70

Stuffed Cabbage

cooking time 1¾ hr

utensils
  kettle
  saucepan
  mixing bowl
  grater
serves 6

BEEF STUFFING
2 lb ground beef
3 slices bread, crust removed
1 cup milk
1 small onion, grated
2 slightly beaten eggs
salt to taste
pinch of ground allspice
1 loose-leafed cabbage

SAUCE
2 cans tomato sauce
2 cups water
juice from 3 lemons to taste
sugar to taste
4 bay leaves
4 allspice
salt and pepper
2 apples cut in quarters
½ cup raisins

Boil cabbage about 15-20 min until tender. Remove from water, cool, and separate leaves with sharp knife; thin thick ribs.

Combine all sauce ingredients except apples and raisins. Bring to boil and simmer.

Mix milk with bread until combined. Add ground beef, grate onion, add rest of stuffing ingredients, and mix together.

Place some of this filling on each leaf and fold over carefully. Put in sauce; simmer about 1 hr. Add apples and raisins, correct the seasoning and simmer ½ hr more.

Yankee Broiled Steak

Choose a steak 1-2 inches thick, of high-quality beef. Slash fat at edges of meat to prevent curling. Don't cut into steak. Preheat broiler.

Place steak on rack so top of meat is 2-4 inches below source of heat —4 inches for thick steaks. Follow the range manufacturer's directions for operating broiler unit. Broil steak until top is well browned; season. Turn, brown other side. (Stick fork into fat, not steak when turning, or use tongs.)

The table below is a guide to broiling time. Only approximate times can be given, because much depends on the broiler, personal preference in doneness of meat, and the meat itself.

Broiling Time for Steaks (Approximate)

1-inch thick:	Total Time (min)
rare	10
medium	15
well done	20-25
1½-inch thick:	
rare	15
medium	20
well done	25-30
2-inch thick:	
rare	25
medium	35
well done	45-50

Place individual steaks on rack 3 inches from heating unit. Broil according to table. If you are using an electric stove, rub with a little softened butter or brush with this sauce for a delicious barbecued taste: mix 2 tbsp soya sauce with ½ tsp Worcestershire sauce, ½ tsp paprika and ¼ tsp onion powder.

When steak is broiled to your taste, remove to a hot plate, sprinkle salt and grind pepper on, serve at once.

Cut thick broiled steaks into slices, spoon the juice over them. A good steak deserves a sharp knife. You can test whether steak is done to your liking by cutting slit in center to see. Individual steaks are more expensive but the easiest to serve to guests.

a quickie

Flip-over Tenderloin Steaks

cooking time 4-6 min

utensils
skillet
2 spatulas
serves as many as you wish

tenderloin steaks cut into ½-inch thick slices
butter or fat as needed
salt and pepper to taste

Wipe tenderloin dry. Heat skillet with a little butter on medium high heat, until it sizzles. Steaks brown better in very little butter. Add the tenderloins, being careful not to crowd or burn them, browning both sides by flipping over and over to get a beautiful brown outside but a rare inside.

Serve at once on heated plates with sprinkle of salt and pepper. This is the easiest and most delicious way to prepare tenderloin.

a quickie

London Broil
Flank Steak

cooking time 8 min
preheat broiler

utensils
broiling pan with rack
tongs
serves 4

1-1½ lb flank steak as thick as possible, room temperature
1 tbsp softened butter

Wipe steak dry with paper towels. Rub butter on before placing on rack to broil 4 min on each side. Remove to hot platter. With sharp knife cut against grain into diagonal thin slices, each slice overlapping. Spoon juice over slices as you serve them.

For a delicious barbecued taste brush on sauce made of 2 tbsp soya sauce, ½ tsp Worcestershire sauce, ½ tsp paprika and ¼ tsp onion powder.

73

a quickie; freezes well too

Tenderloin
in Cream Sauce

cooking time about 10 min

utensils
    heavy skillet
    heated platter
serves 4-5

10 slices tenderloin, ¼-inch thick, at room
    temperature
2 tbsp fat or more as needed
2 cups beef broth made of dehydrated
    soup as per instructions on box
½ cup dry sherry wine
¼ tsp thyme
1 tbsp ketchup
¼ tsp A-1 sauce
1 (4-oz) can sliced mushrooms
¼ tsp salt to taste
⅛ tsp pepper
3 tbsp butter for butter balls
3 tbsp flour for butter balls
½ cup heavy sweet or sour cream

Wipe steaks dry with paper towels, brown, being careful not to crowd, as they will steam, not brown.
Remove to heated plate before removing any fat in
skillet but leave brownings. Stir in all ingredients
except butter, flour and cream and boil gently 3
min to combine flavors while you mix butter and
flour together to make tiny balls for thickening the
sauce.

Gradually stir in cream, add steak and any juice left on
plate. Heat and serve.

If you use sour cream, off heat add a little sauce to
cream until a good bit has been added, then stir
slowly back into sauce; heat but do not boil, as
sour cream curdles.

A good companion to these steaks is riced potatoes.

Braised Steak, Italian Style

cooking time about 2½ hr

utensils
    skillet with lid
    large saucepan
serves 4

2 lb top round steak, 1 inch thick, room temperature
¾ cup canned vegetable juice (6-oz can)
½ cup dry sherry wine
2 cloves garlic
¼ tsp oregano
⅛ tsp basil
2 tsp sugar
2 cups canned tomatoes
1 bay leaf
1 tbsp fat or more
2 tbsp flour
½ tsp salt
pepper
½ lemon sliced into 6 paper-thin slices
* butter balls (see "Thickenings—How Much and How")

Combine all ingredients except steak down to fat, bring to boil, stir constantly about 2 min, reduce to simmer.

Rub salted flour over steak and brown before pouring sauce over it, arrange lemon slices on top. Bring to boil, reduce to simmer, cover, simmer 2-2½ hr. Correct seasoning, add pepper.

If sauce is thin, add butter balls to make it right consistency, stirring them in over low heat.

a quickie

Breaded Veal Chops

cooking time about 10 min

utensils
skillet
serves **4**

8 rib veal chops
½ tsp salt or more
1 egg mixed with pinch of salt and ½ cup
milk
1 cup bread crumbs
2 tbsp fat
pepper to taste

Sprinkle salt on chops, let set for about 10 min before dipping into egg-milk mixture and then one at a time into bread crumbs. Don't bread them heavily.

Fry chops in heated skillet until beautifully browned but not dry. Add pepper. This will take about 10 min on medium heat.

Chops will be more delicate if you coat them lightly.

a quickie; fix ahead

Veal Chops Mozzarella

cooking time 30 min
preheat oven 350°

utensils
skillet
heatproof baking pan
serves **4**

8 veal chops or 2 veal steaks, ½-inch thick,
membranes removed
2 tbsp fat
1 (10½-oz) can marinara sauce
½ tsp salt
2 tsp sugar
4 tbsp sauterne
1 (6-oz) can vegetable juice
4-oz mozzarella cheese, sliced to cover veal
chops

Fry chops lightly; don't crowd. Fry quickly before removing to heatproof baking pan; set aside.

Heat, stir rest of ingredients except cheese, scraping up the good brownings in skillet after removing any fat remaining. Pour this sauce over chops. Cover with slices of cheese. Bake in oven about 30 min.

Veal
in Marinara Sauce

cooking time about 15 min

utensils
   saucepan
   skillet

serves **4**

8 veal rib chops, ¼-inch thick, room
   temperature
2 tbsp fat to fry chops

MARINARA SAUCE
1 (10½-oz) can marinara sauce
2 tsp sugar
2 tbsp brandy
1 (6-oz) can vegetable juice
2 cloves garlic
2 allspice
1 bay leaf
salt and pepper to taste

Bring to boil all sauce ingredients, reduce to simmer for
   10 min.

Preheat skillet with fat, brown chops with membranes
   removed from outside, being careful not to crowd
   them. Set aside on plate while you remove any fat
   in skillet but not the brownings. Swish sauce in
   brownings. Heat, pour over chops, serve.

This is good served with spaghetti as a side dish. It freezes well.

a quickie; freezes well

Veal
in Vermouth

cooking time 15-20 min

utensils
  skillet
serves 4

8 veal chops or 2 veal steaks, ½-inch thick
2 tbsp fat
1 cup canned or dehydrated onion soup,
    strained
¼ cup dry vermouth
2 tbsp sherry
butter balls (see "Thickenings—How Much
    and How")
¼ cup heavy cream
salt and pepper to taste

Remove membrane around chops, wipe dry, preheat skillet with fat, quickly and lightly brown chops on both sides without crowding. Set aside on plate while you remove any fat in skillet but not the brownings. Stir in soup, vermouth, sherry; scrape up brownings, gradually stir in butter balls to thicken sauce. Off heat stir in cream, add veal with any juice on plate, gently heat 5 min. Correct seasoning. Serve at once.

Quickie Veal in Wine and Sour Cream

cooking time 10 min

utensils
   skillet
   saucepan
serves 4

8 veal chops or 2 veal steaks, ½-inch thick
2 tbsp fat
2 tbps flour
2 cups strained canned or dehydrated onion soup
2 bay leaves
2 allspice
⅓ tsp dried basil
½ tsp paprika
1 tsp sugar
3 tsp strained lemon juice
2 tbsp sherry
3 tbsp sour cream, room temperature

Remove membrane from chops, pound veal after removing bones (veal can be used without pounding).

Brown veal chops and set aside on plate. Remove fat from skillet, leaving brownings in. Mix flour and 4 tbsp onion soup together before adding to rest of ingredients except sour cream. Bring to boil, simmer about 5 min, add chops and any juice on plate, bring back to boil, remove from heat. Combine a little sauce with sour cream, gradually stir back into rest of sauce; heat but don't boil, as sour cream may curdle.

Stuffed Breast of Veal

cooking time 2½-3 hr
  preheat oven 325°

utensils
  grater
  chopper
  mixing bowl
  skillet
  casserole with lid
  aluminum foil
serves 8

meaty breast of veal
2 large onions, sliced
4-6 large bay leaves
10 allspice
1½ tsp salt
2 tbsp butter or margarine, melted
2 tbsp fat to brown veal
6 tbsp white wine or water mixed with 2
  tbsp butter or margarine, melted
aluminum foil

STUFFING
1 cup onion, minced fine
⅓ cup celery, minced fine
⅓ cup carrot, grated
½ cup melted butter or margarine
2 cups fresh bread crumbs or 6 slices of
  Holland rusk, broken into pieces
1 large egg, stirred with fork
¾ tsp salt to taste
pepper to taste

Have veal cut with pocket and bones cut through length-
    wise where attached for ease of carving.

The night before, place veal on large piece of foil, rub
    ½ tsp salt inside veal and brush melted butter
    over meaty side before sprinkling 1 tsp salt over it.
    Arrange bay leaves, allspice and sliced onions
    on this side, then wrap foil carefully around to
    hold everything in place. Put in refrigerator to
    marinate overnight.

Remove from refrigerator long enough to get to room
    temperature.

Make stuffing by frying onions soft but not browned, then
    add to rest of ingredients, tossing lightly. Spoon it
    into veal, being careful not to force stuffing in. Close
    by sewing or use aluminum fasteners. As stuffings
    are highly perishable, to be safe, prepare early,
    refrigerate and wait to stuff veal right before roast-
    ing. As veal pockets are so small, it is advisable
    not to stuff veal, but to put stuffing in buttered

80

metal or heatproof casserole ½ hr before veal is done and bake it. The stuffing and veal will be done at the same time. This stuffing is simply delicious, especially when made with Holland rusk.

Remove foil from veal, brown carefully 20-30 min. Before placing in casserole, meaty side up, place foil on veal, then put lid on. Roast 2¼-2½ hr, basting once in a while. The veal will be juicy and tender. Remove from oven and let rest 20 min before carving.

fix ahead; can be made on top of stove

Savory Cold Veal Roast

cooking time 2-2½ hr
preheat oven 325°

utensils
skillet
casserole with lid
serves 8

4-lb rump veal roast in 1 piece, no bones
8 cups onion soup, strained to cover roast
4 bay leaves
4 allspice
4 carrots
2 stalks and leaves of celery
4 cloves garlic
¾ tsp salt to taste
good grind of pepper
1 tsp paprika
fat to brown veal

Brown, don't burn veal, then place in casserole. Remove fat from skillet but leave brownings, swish them with onion soup, before pouring over veal. Add rest of ingredients, bring to boil, reduce heat, put foil over veal and simmer with lid on until tender or place in oven, roast about 2-2½ hr. Don't overcook, as veal will be stringy or squashy instead of firm and juicy. Let cool in broth. Remove from juice, slice when cold to serve. It can also be served hot.

Be sure to use a good brand of mild onion soup, canned or dehydrated, such as Pierce's, Bon Vivant or Knorr's.

Veal Roll-ups

cooking time ½ hr or more

utensils
  skillet
  cord to tie rolls
  aluminum foil
serves 4

8 veal chops or 2 veal steaks, ¼-inch thick, have butcher cut off bones and pound, removing membrane around chops
2 tbsp fat to fry
enough thin-sliced ham to fit 8 slices of veal
1 pkg dried beef broth dissolved in 2 cups boiling water
1 carrot, grated
1 tsp sugar
1 clove garlic
½ cup dry vermouth
salt and pepper to taste
2 tbsp flour stirred into ¼ cup water
1 tbsp butter

Roll and tie lightly salted chops with ham slices in them. Brown, shaking skillet around not to burn, set aside on plate.

Make sauce with rest of ingredients, stirring up brownings; cook, stir 1 min. Return veal to skillet. Place aluminum foil over skillet before putting lid on, simmer about ½ hr or more until tender. Adjust seasoning.

The foil will keep water from dripping on veal. This dish is nice served with noodles or riced potatoes.

Maria's Polish Veal Cutlettes

cooking time 10-12 min

utensils
    mixing bowl
    skillet (teflon preferred)
makes 4 large cutlettes

1 lb ground veal
1 egg, medium size
1 yolk
1 large hard roll softened in cup milk
1 small onion, minced fine
1-2 tbsp butter to soften onion
salt to taste
pepper to taste (veal needs it)
about ½ cup fine fresh bread crumbs
2 tbsp butter to brown cutlettes

Soften roll in milk, mix with your fingers until thoroughly combined.

On medium heat, soften onions in butter without browning.

Combine all ingredients except bread crumbs with ground veal, tasting to correct seasoning. Mix with your fingers, thoroughly working mixture until it feels light.

Shape into 4 large, thick, oblong cakes, roll very lightly in crumbs.

Brown in 2 tbsp butter on both sides, being careful not to burn, on medium-high heat, reduce heat to low, put lid on, sauté 10 min. Don't remove lid while sautéing.

The juice actually spurts out, this is so tender and juicy. It has a delectable taste. Be sure to heat serving plates.

These cutlettes are deluxe hamburgers to us.

fix ahead; can be made on top of stove

Lamb Stew Special

cooking time about 1 hr 45 min
    preheat broiler
    preheat oven 450°

utensils
    broiler
    casserole with lid
    skillet
    saucepan
serves 8

4 lb shoulder of lamb, cut into 2-2½-inch
    pieces
4 tbsp melted butter or margarine
1½ tbsp sugar
5 carrots, peeled, cut into 2-inch pieces
6 tbsp flour
4 cups canned or dehydrated onion soup
    strained
3 cloves garlic
2 large bay leaves
¼ tsp thyme
18 very small new potatoes, peeled
1½ tsp salt to taste
pepper to taste

Brush lamb with melted butter, broil. Brown on both sides without crowding until all have been browned. Set aside in casserole.

Sprinkle sugar over carrots in skillet and glaze 2 min by shaking skillet with 1 tbsp fat.

Sprinkle 3 tbsp flour over lamb, heat in oven 5 min before turning over, sprinkling other side with flour and browning 5 min. Heat onion soup, add to lamb with garlic, thyme, bay leaves, reduce heat to 325°, let bubble gently with lid on 1 hr, adding salt to taste. Place glazed carrots, potatoes in casserole. Correct seasoning, put aluminum foil on before replacing lid so water will not drip into stew. Continue cooking about 45 min. Serve with crusty French or Italian bread.

Be sure to use a good brand of mild onion soup, canned or dehydrated, such as Pierce's, Bon Vivant or Knorr's. If using the latter, add ¼ cup dry sherry.

Broiled Lamb Chops

cooking time 8 min
   preheat broiler 30 min

utensils
   broiler with rack
serves 4

8 thick-cut lamb chops, room temperature
salt and pepper to taste

- Cut 1-rib-thick chops as thick as possible without cutting into double chops.

- For electric broiler, brush some fat, either butter or margarine, to help brown chops. Broil close to unit 4 min on each side. Serve on heated plates.

- For a different taste, brush lamb chops with sauce made of 2 tbsp soy sauce, ½ tsp Worcestershire sauce, ½ tsp paprika, ¼ tsp onion powder. This gives chops a charcoal taste.

can be prepared ahead

Marinated Lamb Chops

cooking time 8 min

utensils
   broiler with rack
   mixing bowl
serves 4

8 single lamb chops, cut thick as possible
2 tbsp butter or margarine melted

MARINATING SAUCE
½ cup vegetable oil
2 tbsp wine vinegar or distilled white vinegar
1 tsp salt
¼ tsp pepper to taste
2 cloves garlic
½ cup dry white wine
½ tsp thyme

- Combine all ingredients for sauce in mixing bowl that fits chops. Marinate chops several hr, wipe dry, brush with melted butter or margarine before broiling 4 min on each side. Serve at once on hot plates.

- You can vary sauce by using ½ cup vegetable oil, juice from 2 lemons, 2 cloves garlic, salt and pepper to taste.

If you use an electric broiler, be sure to preheat it to ensure proper browning.

85

prepare ahead

Gingered Lamb's Leg

cooking time 2-2½ hr
preheat oven 400°

utensils
shallow roaster
rack
bulb baster
foil
serves 8

Leg of lamb, room temperature
4 tbsp butter or margarine, softened
1 tsp salt
2 large onions, sliced
4 cloves garlic, sliced
½ tsp ginger
½ cup dry white wine
4 tbsp butter or margarine added to wine

Overnight, marinate lamb with butter rubbed on, arrange onion slices and garlic on lamb, hold in place by wrapping in aluminum foil. Place in refrigerator.

Next day bring lamb to room temperature, removing onion and garlic. Rub ginger on before placing on rack in roaster. Roast about 2-2½ hr, basting often with wine-butter mixture, not with pan drippings, using bulb baster if you have it. Sprinkle salt the last half-hour. The lamb should be nicely browned, juicy pink inside.

Carve the lamb across top into thin slices. Use sharp knife.

Sizzling Spareribs

cooking time about 1 hr 25 min
    preheat oven 400°

utensils
    blender or mixing bowl
    broiler with rack
    brush for basting
    tongs
    scissors
serves 4

4 racks spareribs, about 10-inch each (if frozen, don't defrost)
2 tsp salt

SAUCE
1 cup vegetable oil
1 cup honey
1 tsp garlic powder
½ tsp onion powder
¼ tsp ginger
¼ cup white vinegar
¼ cup soy sauce
¼ cup sherry wine

Blend all sauce ingredients in blender a second, then 5-6 times off and on, and the sauce is ready, or combine and mix well with spoon. Use as much sauce as you need, save rest for another time in refrigerator.

Sprinkle salt on ribs, place on rack, meaty side up, bake 30 min, reduce heat to 350°, bake other side 30 min. Brush sauce on, bake 10 min, turn meaty side up, brush sauce on, basting twice while baking 15 min. The ribs will be tender, moist, and have a lovely glaze.

Cut with scissors and serve at once.

Some people like hot English mustard with the ribs.

Sherried Pork Patties

cooking time 10 min

utensils
   skillet
serves 4

2 lb ground pork
1 tsp salt to taste
4 tbsp dry sherry
2 tsp grated onions
pepper to taste
2 tbsp fat as needed
2 tbsp finely minced parsley

Combine all ingredients except parsley and fat. Shape into 8 oblong cakes, fry quickly on both sides until browned nicely, reduce heat to low, sauté about 10 min until cakes are well done but still juicy, turning once in a while. Remove fat as it accumulates. Serve on heated plate with minced parsley sprinkled on each cake.

Skewered Pork Chops

cooking time 1 hr or more
   preheat oven 350°

utensils
   skillet
   casserole with lid
   skewer
serves 4

8 center-cut loin pork chops, 1-inch thick
2 tbsp fat to fry
salt and pepper to taste
1 cup cold tap water to cover bottom of casserole about 1 inch

Brown chops nicely, salt and pepper them before pushing skewer through middle of each chop; bone side down, fat side up. Push them together to keep chops from drying out. Bake in casserole with lid on 1 hr. Test for tenderness; if necessary bake 10-15 more min.

Served with skewer, chops look intriguing. Remove one at a time to serve. Defat sauce and serve with chops.

This can be varied by heating can of sauerkraut, placing it around chops, allowing about 35-40 min to cook with chops.

a quickie

Fried Pork Chops, Pennsylvania-Dutch Style

cooking time 45 min

utensils
    skillet with lid
serves 4

8 loin pork chops, ½-inch thick
salt and pepper to taste
about 1 tbsp vegetable shortening
¼ cup hot water

Salt chops and let marinate 20 min or more to season them.

Heat skillet with shortening before putting in chops without crowding, brown on both sides (this takes about 25 min). Add ¼ cup hot water, put lid on, simmer about 20 min, until water evaporates. Serve on heated plates and sprinkle pepper on.

These can be varied by poaching in ¼ cup vermouth instead of hot water.

```
HAM
```

fix ahead

Homemade Canned Ham

cooking time about 2½ hr
    preheat oven 300°

utensils
    broiling pan with rack
serves 8 or more

3-lb canned ham, firm type
½ cup dry sherry wine
½ cup honey (orange blossom is good)

Pour a little sherry over ham placed on rack in broiling pan. Baste every 10 min while it bakes 2 hr in oven, turning over after it has baked 1 hr.

Increase heat to 400°, spoon honey on one side and glaze 15 min before doing same to other side.

This ham is delicious served either hot or cold and should be sliced very thin. You can vary the taste of the ham by basting with pineapple juice instead of sherry. Creamed spinach goes well with ham.

fix ahead; delicious hot or cold

Poached Ham
in Orange Wine

cooking time 1 hr 6 min.

utensils
    saucepan
    broiler
serves 2, 3-lb ham serves 6-8

1-lb Plumrose Danish canned ham
    or
3-lb ham (tender all-meat hams are excellent)
2 cloves for 1-lb ham; 6 for 3-lb ham
half and half orange wine, vermouth or sherry mixed with water, to cover ham when poaching
¼ cup honey and 1-2 tbsp orange wine to glaze 1-lb ham (double quantity for 3-lb ham)

Bring to boil, reduce heat to simmer 1 hr to poach ham. Poach 3-lb ham 2 hr.

Brush with honey-orange wine mixture, and glaze in broiler, 3 min on each side.

a quickie

Sautéed Calves' Liver on Rice

cooking time 15-20 min

utensils
  saucepan with lid
serves 4

*prepare rice by cooking "Rice—The French Method" (see its recipe)
8 slices of cubed calves' liver, ½-inch thick, room temperature, membranes removed
4 medium onions, minced
4 tbsp fat
salt and pepper to taste

On high heat brown lightly but don't burn onions in fat; reduce heat to do this. Keep stirring and don't go away. When onions are soft and beautifully browned, add cubed liver all at once. Stir, shake to cook liver, add salt and pepper to taste (this takes about 5 min); then put lid on for 1 min. Serve at once over rice.

a quickie

Chicken Livers in Vermouth

cooking time 25 min

utensils
    skillet
serves **4**

1 lb fresh chicken livers
about 2 tbsp fat
1 large onion, minced
2 cans chicken broth
2 tsp tomato sauce
8 drops tabasco
4 tbsp (¼ cup) vermouth
½ tsp Accent
*butter balls (see "Thickenings—How Much and How")
salt to taste

Brown onion, don't burn, set aside on plate.

Brown livers very lightly, barely browning. The livers should be pink inside (you will cook them more later). Remove from skillet, set aside.

Remove fat from skillet, leave brownings. Swish chicken broth into brownings before adding rest of ingredients except butter balls. Bring to boil, reduce to simmer. Simmer 10 min before dropping in butter balls to thicken. Add livers, bring back to boil, simmer a few min, so livers won't get dry. Correct seasoning. Serve.

This dish keeps quite well, up to 1 hr if necessary, over hot water, especially if you don't cook livers past the pink stage. It freezes well.

Spiced Roast Duck

cooking time 2-2½ hr
  preheat oven 400°-450°
  Reduce to 350° when
    you put duck in.

utensils
  shallow roaster with rack
serves 2-4, depending on ap-
    petites

1 duck, 4½-5½ lb, Long Island type, de-
    frosted, wiped dry inside and out,
    room temperature
2 tbsp softened, not melted butter or mar-
    garine to smear over duck
1 tsp salt (¼ tsp for inside, ¼ tsp for
    back, ½ tsp for breast and front of
    duck)
1 large onion, peeled and sliced thin
6 bay leaves
12 allspice

The day before roasting defrosted duck, place on large
  sheet of foil, rub butter over duck and salt it.
  Arrange bay leaves, allspice, onion slices on duck,
  holding in place with the butter. Wrap foil completely around duck so seasonings are held in place
  before putting in refrigerator to marinate overnight.

A few hours before roasting, remove duck to get to
  room temperature. Put seasonings inside duck, reduce heat to 350°, place duck on rack in roaster,
  breast side up, roast 30 min. Stick with sharp
  prongs of fork to help fat escape every half hour.
  Turn breast down, roast 45 min, then breast up
  30 min. Roast breast down 30 min, breast up 15
  min. The duck should be browned and tender. Test
  to see if done by raising duck. If juice runs out
  yellow, duck is cooked; if it is pink, continue
  roasting and check at 5-min intervals.

When duck is cooked, remove fat. If duck isn't brown
  enough, place duck on rack and broil, back up,
  about 2 min or more; turn over, broil breast up
  2-3 min. This crisps the duck's skin to make it
  more delicious and a beautiful brown color. Usually
  this is not necessary.

The Long Island ducks have a tremendous amount of
  fat and roasting them on a rack is the best solution.

*You can make "Black Cherry Sauce" (see its recipe), to give a different
fruited taste to duck. "Potato Cakes" (see their recipe) go well with
duck, also apple sauce, as does sauerkraut in wine (see "Gourmet Sauerkraut"), but only when you spice the duck. The cherry sauce is rich
and sweet and needs new potatoes sautéed in butter, and crisp, fresh
broccoli and a cucumber salad in vinaigrette sauce.*

93

Roast Turkey

Preheat oven 450°

It is difficult to say exactly how long it takes to roast a turkey properly, because turkeys may be fed differently, which necessitates longer or shorter cooking time. Whether the turkey is fresh or frozen, whether it is right from the refrigerator or at room temperature— all this has to be taken into consideration. The nice thing about roasting a turkey is that whatever method you use, unless you overcook it to a dull dryness, it will be delicious. We have roasted small ones, large ones, with a lid, without a lid, in a shallow roaster, in aluminum foil, and have been successful. I have come to the conclusion there's just not one way to roast a turkey.

We do have opinions on what size turkey and what kind to roast. We prefer hen turkeys 12-lb and under. If you are having a large group, buy two hen turkeys and have deliciously tender flavor, rather than a large one. The texture of a large turkey never is delicate to our taste.

And now some of the ways to roast a turkey. Our favorite is to get the 12-lb turkey to room temperature. If it is frozen defrost it to room temperature, wipe and salt both inside and outside very well. While it is getting to room temperature, it has a chance to have the salt go through it and give the turkey a taste which it cannot get any other way as well. When it is room temperature, smear softened butter inside and out. Cover legs, part of breast and neck that you have stuffed, wings and back with foil to keep from burning. Be sure to cover these parts with foil before you place in oven; it stays on better and you won't burn yourself doing it later. Place on rack breast down, and brown 15 min in preheated 450° oven. Turn breast up, and brown 15 min. Baste with melted butter. Reduce heat to 325°, turn breast down, roast 1½ hr, basting back once in a while. Turn breast up, baste and roast 1 hr, basting now and then with melted butter. Test to see if turkey is done by moving leg, if it moves easily, it is ready. Also, you can raise turkey up, if juice is yellow and not pink, it is done. When stuffed, punch on bony bottom of back near thigh to see if juice is yellow. This is a foolproof way not to overcook.

Let rest outside oven about 20-30 min for juices to spread themselves and make carving easier.

APPROXIMATE ROASTING TIMES FOR TURKEY AT ROOM TEMPERATURE

weight	min/lb	total time
6 lb	20	2 hr
7 lb	20	2 hr 20 min
8 lb	19	2 hr 30 min
9 lb	18	2 hr 42 min
10 lb	17	2 hr 52 min
11 lb	16	2 hr 56 min
12 lb	15	3 hr
16 lb	14	3 hr 45 min

It takes about 3 lb dressing for a 10-lb bird, 4 lb for a 15-lb bird.

Don't stuff bird until roasting time. You can make stuffing early, but be sure to refrigerate it until ready to roast turkey.

See "Stuffing for Chicken, Turkey, or Veal" in this chapter.

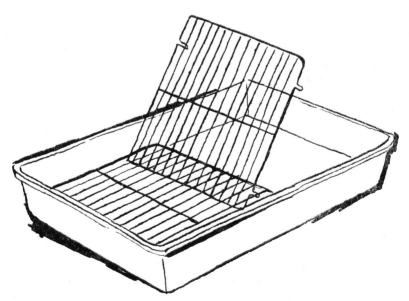

HOMEMADE BROILING PAN. Put one or two racks in shallow roasting pan to make your broiling pan—perfect to roast ducks, broil steaks, chickens, bacon and lamb chops.

95

Roast Goose

cooking time 2½-2¾ hr
preheat oven 425°

utensils
roaster and rack
fork with sharp prongs
sheet of foil large enough
to enclose goose
serves 6-8

1 (9½-10½ lb) frozen goose, defrosted one
day, spiced next day, roasted third day
5 bay leaves broken in halves or thirds
10-12 allspice
2 large onions, 1 whole, 1 sliced
2-3 cloves garlic, sliced
1 tsp salt for outside goose
½ tsp salt for inside goose
about 2 tbsp butter or margarine softened
to room temperature, not melted
pepper

Place defrosted, wiped goose on foil. Put whole onion
into goose, salt it inside and outside. Dab butter
on and place onion, garlic, bay leaves and allspice
on goose, butter holds them in place. Wrap foil
around goose so spices won't fall off. Place in
refrigerator to dry marinate overnight.

Next day let stand 4-6 hr to get to room temperature.

Remove spices, put them and onion inside goose, place
goose breast down on rack, roast 15 min, place
breast up 15 min, reduce heat to 350°, depending
on your oven, roast breast down 1 hr, baste with
boiling water to cut grease, also punch holes in
skin, not meat, to release fat, turn breast up, roast
¾-1 hr, continuing as before until goose has
roasted 2½ hr. Test by tilting goose up; if juice
runs clear, "your goose is cooked," if it runs pink-
ish, roast another 5-10 min and test. Remove
from oven. For beautiful crisp skin, remove fat,
after taking out of oven, place on rack and broil
each side until goose is beautiful brown color.
Then let it rest 20 min to make carving easier.

*We do not like to stuff goose because the dressing seems too greasy;
we also prefer not to stuff it with prunes or apples, as they permeate
goose and take away that special goose taste. We do like to serve apple
sauce with tangy lemon juice in it, or poached prunes filled with walnuts
marinated in brandy, or fried apple rings, and by all means "Potato
Cakes" (see their recipe) made of raw grated potatoes, crisp and delicious. Also, a dish of sauerkraut cooked with white wine and juniper
berries is not to be sneezed at (see "Gourmet Sauerkraut").*

Juicy Roasted Chicken

baking time 1 hr 15 or 20 min
preheat oven 450°

utensils
shallow roaster with rack
serves 4

3½-lb fryer, wiped dry, room temperature
1 tbsp softened butter or soft margarine to smear inside chicken
¼ tsp salt for inside chicken
1 tbsp softened butter or soft margarine to smear outside chicken
¾ tsp salt for outside chicken

Place chicken breast down, bake 15 min in preheated oven. Turn breast up, bake 15 min. Reduce heat to 325°, baste breast before turning it down and bake 25 min. Turn breast up, baste, bake 25 min for luscious crisp tender skin and juicy chicken. Test chicken for doneness by tilting; if juice is yellow or colorless, not pink, chicken is ready. Also, if leg moves easily, it is done. Checking juice is the best method.

Remove from oven, let stand 10-15 min for juices to spread and for easier carving.

Approximate Roasting Times for Chicken

weight	time
1½ lb	45 min
2½-2¾ lb	1 hr 10 min
3 lb	1 hr 15 min
3½ lb	1 hr 20 min

Ahead-of-Time
Fried Chicken

cooking time time to fry and
55 min to bake
preheat oven 325°

utensils
large plate or paper bag
skillet
baking dish with rack
tongs
serves 4-6

Disjoint 2 2½-lb fryers at room temperature each into 2 drumsticks, 2 thighs, 2 breast halves cut lengthwise 2 wings and 2 backs. Dry thoroughly and season with 1 tsp salt.

Put 1 cup or more all-purpose flour, as needed, seasoned with ½ tsp salt, in heavy paper bag or on large plate, set aside.

Add ½ cup milk to 1 extra large egg mixed with pinch of salt.

Melt 2 cups or more vegetable shortening to make 1½ inches fat in skillet. Add ¼ cup butter (the secret that makes the chicken a golden yellow and adds a special flavor).

While shortening and butter are melting on high heat, dip chicken into egg mixture, one piece at a time; shake in paper bag or dip into seasoned flour on plate until well coated. Continue until all are dipped and coated.

Test fat by dropping small piece of bread; if it rises instantly and starts to brown, it is ready to receive the chicken parts, meaty side down, not crowded

98

so they brown quickly and evenly. Reduce to medium high if necessary. Turn chicken with tongs so it browns evenly on both sides. Be careful not to overbrown or burn; the chicken should be golden brown.

As each piece browns, remove with tongs, place on paper towels to drain off fat. When all have been fried and drained, place cooled thighs and drumsticks on metal rack in shallow baking dish in one layer. Save wings, breasts and backs to put in a little later. Close baking dish tightly with aluminum foil. You can finish chicken now or later. Frying chicken earlier and finishing later is a 2-step method that makes for easier cooking.

Place chicken in preheated 325° oven, bake 15 min, lift off foil to add rest of chicken; be sure to close foil before baking 30 more min—45 min total time. If there is no room for the additional chicken, put it in another shallow pan on rack, be sure to cover with foil, bake with rest of chicken.

After baking 45 min total time, remove foil, turn heat up to 400°, and bake 10 min uncovered to crisp the chicken.

This is a good dish for guests as the hostess cook can do all of the work in the morning and be fresh and cheerful for her guests. This fried chicken is delicious cold and wonderful for a picnic.

Buttered Broiled or Barbecued Chicken

cooking time 25-30 min
  preheat broiler

utensils
  broiling pan with rack
  pair of tongs
  basting brush with natural
    bristles
serves 2

Select a broiling chicken, 1½-2 lb.

Sprinkle ¾ tsp salt on chicken while getting it to room temperature.

Brush 2 tbsp melted butter or margarine on both sides of salted chicken, place bony side up on broiler rack, 3 inches from heat. When browned, move lower so chicken will not burn and broil 10-15 min. With tongs turn chicken skin side up, baste, broil 3 inches from heat until lightly browned, lower pan, continue to broil 10-15 min. Don't overcook; smaller chickens cook very fast. Cut into chicken near bone to see if it is cooked. The chicken should be crisp outside and juicy inside.

You can vary this by using our "Basting Sauce for Broiled Chicken or Fish" (see its recipe). Be sure to try it. These chickens are delicious served cold, especially the small ones. Be sure the chicken is cooked, there's nothing worse than a raw chicken; on the other hand there's nothing worse than a dried out overcooked chicken. Broiled chickens need careful watching, but there's nothing more delicious and easy to make.

You can barbecue chicken or Cornish hen by daubing barbecue sauce on thickly. Daub sauce only once on each side to keep the skin from getting sticky. Here is the sauce: Combine in jar and shake ¼ tsp dried mustard, ½ cup ketchup, ¼ cup sweet pickle juice, ¼ cup vegetable oil, ¼ cup Worcestershire sauce, ¼ cup prepared mustard, ¼ cup honey, juice from 1 lemon, and few drops tobasco sauce.

Another good way to barbecue chicken is to daub once on each side with "Southern Barbecue Sauce" (see its recipe). Put foil over chicken to keep from burning.

100

Flavory Chicken Pies

advance preparation time
  soup: 1 hr 15 min
  piecrust dough: 10 min
baking time 30 min
  preheat oven 450°

utensils
  saucepan
  bowl for mixing dough
  4 individual casseroles
  baking sheet

*dough for 1-crust "Rosa's Old-fashioned Piecrust" (see its recipe)
*"Mama's Chicken Noodle Soup" (see its recipe), made without the noodles
1 carrot, diced, blanched in salted water
¼ cup celery, blanched in salted water
½ cup fresh or canned mushrooms, sautéed in 1 tbsp fat
½ cup fresh peas, blanched, or frozen peas, banged on edge of table or board to separate
6 tbsp flour
salt and pepper to taste

Roll dough into ball, set aside in refrigerator.

Let chicken cool in broth. Remove chicken from broth. Cut cold chicken into cubes, divide into casseroles, mix in vegetables, set aside.

Mix flour into 6 tbsp broth, gradually stir into 3¾ cups broth, bring to boil, reduce heat, stir, cook until thickened, about 5 min. Season to taste. Divide into casseroles.

Remove dough from refrigerator, divide into 4 portions, roll out 1 at a time, fit on each casserole; to seal edges, press down with fork. Cut 4 good slits in each crust to vent steam, so crust won't get soggy.

Place on baking sheet in preheated oven, bake 30 min until nicely browned.

Chicken pies freeze well, unbaked. Bake frozen pies 50-60 min. These pies sound hard, but are very easy to make. You can double the recipe and eat one, freeze one.

Chicken
in Champagne Sauce

baking time about 45 min
  preheat oven 450°

utensils
  shallow roasting pan with
    rack
  saucepan
  strainer
  brush for basting
serves 4

2 (2½-lb) chickens, room temperature,
  wipe dry with paper towels
2 tsp salt (¼ tsp for inside, ¾ tsp for
  outside each chicken)
4 tsp softened butter or margarine (1 tsp
  smeared inside and outside each
  chicken)
1 tbsp melted butter or margarine to baste

CHAMPAGNE SAUCE

1 lb fresh whole very small mushrooms,
  wiped clean
2-4 tbsp butter or margarine to saute mushrooms
1 cup chicken broth, fresh or canned
1 cup thick whipping cream
¾ cup champagne (French if possible)
butter balls (see "Thickening—How Much
  and How")

COMPLEMENTARY VEGETABLES

*"Deep South Yellow Grits" (see its recipe)
fresh green asparagus or fresh sweet peas
*golden seedless raisins, steamed (see
  "Steaming" and "Tested Times for
  Steaming Vegetables")
bibb lettuce salad in *"Vinaigrette Sauce"
  (see its recipe)

In the preheated oven bake buttered, salted chickens, breast down 15 min, baste once, turn breast up, bake 15 min, reduce heat to 325°, baste breast, turn down, bake 15 min, turn breast up about 2 min. Test by tilting chickens. If juice running out is yellow, it is done; if pink, bake a few min longer and test again.

Remove from oven, let stand 10 min to make carving easier and enable juices to spread. Save roasting pan.

While chickens rest, make champagne sauce. Sauté the mushrooms in butter, set aside. Remove any fat

102

from roasting pan, on medium heat swish chicken broth around to get all the good taste out of the brownings, cook 2 min, strain. Gradually stir in on medium heat the cream, then the champagne; thicken with some butter balls to get right consistency. Add mushrooms; keep hot.

Meanwhile, cut chickens in half lengthwise, place on heated platter, spoon sauce with mushrooms over them; arrange yellow grits, green asparagus or peas, and golden yellow steamed raisins as attractively as you can. This should be a beautiful dish to look at as well as to eat.

fix ahead

Smothered Chicken

cooking time 1½-2 hr
    preheat broiler

utensils
    casserole with lid
    broiling pan, no rack
serves 3-4

Cut a 2½- or 3-lb fryer at room temperature into quarters, cut breast lengthwise in half, separate drumsticks from thighs, wipe dry, season with 1 tsp salt.

Brush both sides of chicken with 2 tbsp melted butter or margarine before placing in broiling pan, brown 3 inches from heat, skin side up first. Place seasoned chicken in casserole, skin side down, dot with 2 tbsp butter or margarine, arrange large onion cut into ¼-inch thick slices on top. Cover with lid, place on high heat until steam appears. Then reduce heat to simmer, simmer 1½-2 hr.

While chicken is cooking, prepare *"Rice—The French Method" (see its recipe). When chicken is tender, remove onion, squeeze as much juice from it as you can, combine with gravy in casserole, pour over rice and chicken. If there isn't enough gravy, add some canned chicken broth.

103

tastes as good as it sounds

Chicken Veronique

roasting time about 45 min
preheat oven 450°

utensils
shallow roasting pan with
rack
saucepan
strainer
serves 4

2 (2- or 2½-lb) plump chickens, room
temperature, wiped dry
4 tsp softened butter or margarine (1 tsp
smeared inside and outside each
chicken)
2 tsp salt (½ tsp for inside each chicken,
½ tsp for outside each chicken)
about 1 tbsp melted butter to baste chickens

VERONIQUE SAUCE
1 8-oz can whole very small mushrooms
1 cup fresh or canned chicken broth
1 cup thick whipping cream
¾ cup dry vermouth
*butter balls (see "Thickenings—How Much
and How")

VEGETABLES TO GARNISH PLATTER
*"Risotto—Baked in the Oven" (see its
recipe)
1 lb canned green grapes

Bake buttered, salted chickens, breast down, 15 min,
baste, bake breast up 15 min, baste, reduce heat
to 325°, turn breast down, bake 15 min, turn
breast up for about 2 min.

Test by tilting chicken, checking color of the juice that
runs out. If it is clear yellow, it is done; if pink,
continue to bake 5 min more and test.

Remove chicken to a heated platter, save roasting pan,
let chicken rest 10 min to distribute juice and
make carving easier. Make Veronique sauce as
follows.

Remove fat from roasting pan, being careful to leave
brownings. On heat stir in chicken broth, scraping
in good brownings to add flavor. Cook about 3
min, strain, put in saucepan, add cream, bring to
boil, reduce heat, cook about 2 min before adding
vermouth, bring back to boil, reduce heat, simmer

104

about 5 min to combine flavors, adding butter balls to chicken sauce just enough to have body. Add mushrooms.

Heat grapes, while cutting chicken. Cut chickens in half lengthwise, place on heated platter, spoon sauce and mushrooms over, arrange attractively the grapes removed with slotted spoon and risotto.

When you serve chicken Veronique you should dine out at home with your favorite man and your favorite friends. The chicken baked in this manner is tender, juicy and has a delectable flavor.

good for leftover chicken

Creamed Chicken, or Chicken à la King

cooking time about 10 min

utensils
  saucepan
serves 4

4 cups diced cooked chicken
1 can mushroom soup
1 chicken bouillon cube
½ cup cream or milk
2 egg yolks
1 can button mushrooms, strained
2-3 tbsp dry sherry to taste
1 canned pimento, diced
pepper to taste

Stir cream or milk gradually into mushroom soup until it is smooth. Heat, add sherry, stir bouillon cube in before adding chicken, mushrooms. Add pimento, heat, stir in egg yolks, off heat, being careful not to boil when you put mixture back on heat, as it may curdle. Correct seasoning. Serve over crisp toast or in shells (prebaked, frozen or bought from good bakery) that have been baked and are hot when you spoon the chicken à la king in them.

Chicken, Spanish Style

cooking time about 2 hr

utensils
    casserole with lid
    skillet
    basting brush with natural
      bristles

serves 4

*"Steamed Rice" (see its recipe)
2½- or 3-lb fryer
2 tbsp fat to brown fryer
2 cups (2 8-oz cans) tomato sauce
3-4 drops tabasco
¼ cup onions, diced
¼ cup green pepper, diced
1 tbsp diced celery
½ tsp dried oregano
½ tsp sugar
pepper and salt to taste
¼ cup butter or margarine to dot chicken
    in casserole

Cut fryer at room temperature into quarters, cut breast in half lengthwise, separate legs from thighs, wipe dry.

Brown chicken in fat, meat side down in skillet, place in casserole. Remove the fat from skillet but leave brownings. Add tomato sauce, scraping in the good brownings. Add tabasco while heating, then add rest of ingredients, stir, cook until sauce boils. Correct seasoning.

Pour sauce over chicken, dot with butter. Grind pepper over, put lid on, bring to boil until steam appears, then lower heat to simmer, simmer about 1½ hr. Correct seasoning. Serve with rice.

106

Chicken Chow Mein

cooking time about 10 min

utensils
    skillet
    wooden spoon
serves 4-5

1 cup "Steamed Rice" (see its recipe)
4 cups cooked chicken, cut into bite-size pieces
1-2 chicken bouillon cubes
2 stalks celery, diced, blanched in boiling water
4 green onions, minced
1 (1-lb) can chow mein noodles, opened, set aside to eliminate canned taste
1 (1-lb) can Chinese vegetables
1 (1-lb) can chop suey vegetables
1 small can water chestnuts, drained and sliced
1 small can bamboo shoots, drained
1 cup canned or fresh chicken broth, more if needed
1½ tbsp cornstarch mixed with 2 tbsp chicken broth
½ tsp Accent (optional)
salt to taste
½ cup canned almonds, peeled, sliced
soy sauce

Combine all vegetables with chicken broth and bouillon cube, bring to boil, add chicken, bring back to boil, add, stir, cook cornstarch mixture until it is clear and has body; this takes about 5 min. Correct seasoning, taste, add additional chicken bouillon cube if necessary. Add almonds, heat thoroughly.

Serve over the rice, pass noodles. Most people like to put some soy sauce over chow mein.

no cooking

Sherried Stuffed Prunes

serves as many as you wish

large, tender fresh prunes with seeds removed
walnuts or pecan halves
cream sherry to marinate prunes

Stuff prunes, place in bowl to fit so you won't waste sherry. Cover with sherry and marinate 4 hr in refrigerator. Serve as garnish with goose, chicken, ducks, Cornish hens, and what could be finer with a rib roast?

If you care to bring prunes and sherry to a boil, reduce to simmer, poach 1 min. Remove from heat, let cool, refrigerate until needed.

I suggest Almeden's Solera cream sherry because it is delicious with prunes, and it is inexpensive.

Stuffing for Chicken, Turkey or Veal

utensils
skillet
large mixing bowl
rubber spatula
spoon

⅓ cup finely minced celery
1 cup finely minced onion or frozen chopped onion
⅓ cup grated carrot
½ cup melted butter or margarine
2 cups bread crumbs or 6 slices Holland rusk, broken in pieces
1 large egg, stirred with fork
¾ tsp salt to taste
pepper to taste

Fry onion in butter on medium heat, stirring until soft, being careful not to brown. Combine all ingredients in bowl and toss together lightly. Spoon it into cavity, being careful not to force stuffing in, but keep it light. Close by either sewing with large needle and thread, or using aluminum fasteners.

As stuffing is highly perishable, to be safe you can prepare it early and refrigerate; but wait to stuff your fowl or meat right before baking it.

For a 10-12-lb turkey, the quantities in the recipe above should be increased 2½ times.

one of the best, easiest ways to cook vegetables

Steaming

The U.S. Department of Agriculture's Research Department says that steaming is one of the two best methods to retain nutrients in vegetables and I can add it is also the best method to retain both the beautiful natural colors, whether bright green or otherwise, and retain the best natural individual vegetable flavors.

If you like vegetables to taste as they should, look as beautifully green as when they were picked, then by all means use my steaming method as described under the illustrations of steamers—not the pressure cooker though, because a pressure cooker tends to make vegetables mushy and overcooks them, since it is too hard to control for fragile vegetables.

If you wish to cook ahead be sure to remove the vegetables from the steamer and immediately run cold water over them to stop the cooking. Reheat in a heavy saucepan when ready by moving off and on heat until heated. Please don't keep cooked vegetables over low heat or in a hot saucepan as it only cooks them longer and ruins them.

TESTED TIMES FOR STEAMING VEGETABLES

Vegetables	Approximate Cooking Time
Carrots, whole	15 min
Carrots, sliced	7-10 min
Broccoli heads	8-10 min
Broccoli stalks	12-14 min
Cauliflower	15 min
Spinach	2-4 min
String beans, whole	15 min
String beans, cut	10 min
Peas	5-7 min
Asparagus	7-10 min
Brussels sprouts	7-8 min
Cabbage, cut in quarters	8 min
Potatoes	
Idaho, 4″ x 2½″	1 hr
New potatoes, marble-sized	Start testing at 10 min
New potatoes, 1″	Start testing at 12 min
Large boiling potatoes (waxy type)	
3½″ x 2½″	45-50 min
New potatoes, 1½″	Start testing at 14 min
Sweet potatoes 6″ x 2½″	35-40 min
Squash, cubed	5 min
Whole mushrooms, large	7 min
Whole mushrooms, medium	7 min
Raisins	3 min

Remember size and freshness of vegetables and a person's taste influence the length of cooking time, but by steaming you can always test by tasting whenever you wish.

TESTED TIMES FOR STEAMING FROZEN VEGETABLES
(10 oz pkg)

Frozen Vegetables	Approximate Time (min)	Defrosting Instructions
Limas, Fordhook	9	Defrost only enough to separate. (Takes 7-9 min)
Broccoli heads	5	Defrost enough to separate (takes about 1 hr)
Broccoli stalks	12-14	Takes about ½ hr
Brussels sprouts	7	Needs no defrosting
String beans, cut	7	Needs no defrosting
String beans, whole	7	Takes about 1 hr
Asparagus	4	Cut off tough part; defrost only enough to separate (takes about 1 hr)
Peas	5	Takes about ½ hr
Potatoes 2" x 1½"	15	Needs no defrosting
Spinach	6	Don't defrost

You can defrost vegetables by transfering from freezer to refrigerator in the morning and steaming in time for dinner, or you can defrost by removing from freezer to the kitchen for a shorter period as per the table above. You can also separate frozen vegetables by banging the box on a hard surface. This does the trick, and I like this method best. Stand carton on end and whack it against firm surface or whack with wooden mallet without breaking box. Keep turning box, whacking each side and the other end until all vegetables are broken apart. Be careful not to break box. This really works well and separates vegetables so they cook evenly and quicker.

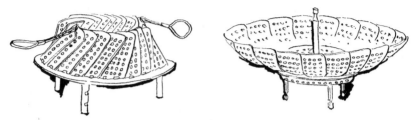

TWO MODERATELY PRICED STEAMERS. Left: inexpensive steamer which works fine but is fragile and has to be replaced after day-by-day usage. **Right:** higher-priced steamer which is more durable and may prove less expensive in the long run. Both of these steamers have to be placed in a large enough saucepot with lid to fit. There is usually one such pot in every kitchen. To use either of these steamers, fill saucepot with 1 qt water, let boil until it steams fast, place vegetables in steamer, put lid on, bring back to fast steam, reduce heat to medium and steam until the vegetables are as you like them, crisp, tender and tasty.

THE BEST STEAMER. Here you have the steamer saucepot right along with the steamer. They are well made to last for many years. This steamer is also very easy to handle, which is a boon with vegetables like peas that roll around, and is easy to remove when vegetables are cooked. This Steamer Flavor Saver can be purchased by mail from Hanover House, Hanover, Pa., for $5.95.

112

the other best way to cook vegetables

Boiling

The other best method for cooking vegetables is to cook with water to cover and cook fast until tender. You can always tell a good cook, for he or she never overcooks vegetables. Vegetables cooked just long enough are naturally bright without additives. See "Tested Times for Boiling Fresh Vegetables." For boiling frozen vegetables, follow the directions on the packages.

TESTED TIMES FOR BOILING FRESH VEGETABLES

Vegetable	Boiling Time (Min)	Vegetable	Boiling Time (Min)
Asparagus		Collards	10-20
whole	10-20	Corn on cob	5-15
tips	5-15	Dandelion greens	10-20
Beans		Kale	10-25
lima	20-25	Kohlrabi, sliced	20-25
snap, 1" pieces	15-30	Okra	10-15
Beets		Onions	15-30
young, whole	30-45	Parsnips	
older, whole	45-90	whole	20-40
sliced or diced	15-25	quartered	10-20
Beet greens, young	5-15	Peas	8-20
Broccoli, heavy		Potatoes	
stalks split	10-15	whole (medium)	25-40
Brussels sprouts	10-20	quartered	20-25
Cabbage		diced	10-15
shredded	3-10	Rutabagas, pared, cut up	20-30
quartered	10-15	Spinach	3-10
Carrots		Squash	
young, whole	15-25	summer, sliced	10-20
older, whole	20-30	winter, cut up	15-20
sliced	10-20	Sweet potatoes, whole	25-35
Cauliflower		Tomatoes, cut up	7-15
separated	8-15	Turnips	
whole	15-20	cut up	10-20
Celery, cut up	15-18	whole	20-30
Chard	10-20	Turnip greens	10-30

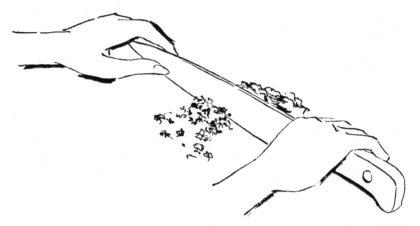

HOW TO HOLD A FRENCH CHEF'S KNIFE. This knife can be the most useful help in your cooking and can be bought at some department stores. To cut or slice vegetables or fruits, grip knife with thumb and index finger of one hand, place fingers of your other hand around handle.

CHOPPING VEGETABLES WITH FRENCH CHEF'S KNIFE. When chopping fruits, vegetables, parsley or chives, hold knife on both ends and, seesaw fashion, chop rapidly. For efficiency, keep pushing ingredients together with knife until desired size is attained.

114

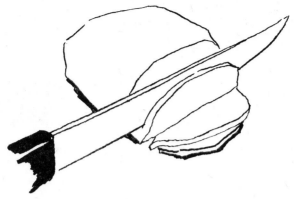

SLICING ROUND VEGETABLES WITH FRENCH CHEF'S KNIFE. When preparing a round fruit or vegetable, such as a potato or onion, cut a thin slice off bottom to keep it flat and steady on your board, or cut through middle and place flat side down on board; hold firmly, pointing your fingers back, and slice to thickness desired.

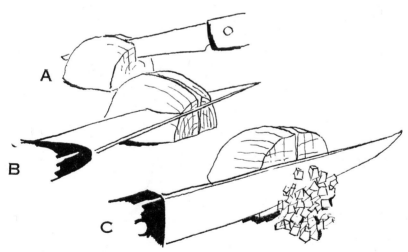

DICING ROUND VEGETABLES WITH FRENCH CHEF'S KNIFE. To dice round vegetables like onions, peel them but leave root attached, slice down middle, put cut side down, root away from you, cut vertical slices from end to root, leaving root attached, as in **A.** Cut horizontal slices from end to root, as in **B;** now cut down crosswise into a dice or mince, as in **C.**

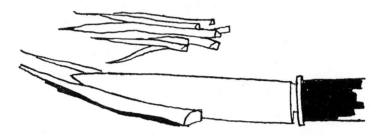

SLICING LONG VEGETABLES WITH FRENCH CHEF'S KNIFE. For slicing long vegetables like carrots into strips, cut down center, face object flat side down, cut into lengthwise strips.

DICING LONG VEGETABLES WITH FRENCH CHEF'S KNIFE. For dicing long vegetables, take same steps as in slicing; then cut crosswise into small pieces.

nothing tastes better

Good Baked Potatoes

baking time 1 hr
  preheat oven 400°

utensils
  baking pan
serves as many as you like

1 Idaho potato per person, washed, cleaned
  thoroughly with vegetable brush
butter or other fat to rub on skin of potato
salt and pepper to taste
lump of butter

Bake in oven 1 hr until potato is soft. Remove from oven, work potato in your hands until it breaks open (using paper towels if necessary); this will make it soft and mealy, really delicious. It can be eaten as is with sprinkle of salt and pepper or add lump of butter.

Never cut a cross in potato thinking this will let steam out and make it mealy—it won't.

can be prepared earlier

Baked Potatoes and Sour Cream

cooking time 1 hr to bake;
  10-15 minutes to reheat
  preheat oven 400°

utensils
  baking pan
serves as many as you wish

1 Idaho potato per person, washed, cleaned
  with vegetable brush
butter to smear skin before baking
½ tsp chopped scallions or chives per potato
chunks of cheddar cheese
2 tbsp sour cream per potato
salt and pepper to taste

When potatoes are baked, scoop out inside, mash with spoon, mix in sour cream, salt, pepper, chopped scallions or chives, place back into shells. Dot with butter and cheddar cheese.

Place in oven to heat and brown (takes 10-15 min)

These potatoes may be baked, stuffed in morning, reheated when ready without loss of flavor. They will take about ½ hr to be thoroughly heated.

117

Steamed Potatoes

cooking time see table

utensils
   steamer and saucepan
serves as many as you wish

small new potatoes
butter (optional)
salt and pepper
sour cream (optional)
sour cream and minced chives (optional)
minced parsley

Potatoes are more "potatofied" when cooked in steamer.
They have a true potato taste. You can serve
"new" potatoes in their skins, or you can peel them.
You can steam them in usual way, heat 4 cups
water to boil, put potatoes in steamer, bring
back to boil, put lid on, steam until done. The
table is below.

Size (inches)	Cooking Time
1-1½	about 20 min
2-2½	25-30 min
3-4	40 min

Here are some ways to serve steamed new potatoes.
While hot, add butter, salt and pepper or serve
with sour cream after peeling potatoes, or add sour
cream and minced chives or green scallions, or
roll in melted butter and minced parsley after peeling the boiled little potatoes. These little new potatoes are good to eat with the skins on, too.

Riced Potatoes

cooking time 25 min

utensils
    saucepan
    ricer
serves as many as you wish

Boil Idaho potatoes, peeled and cut in half, in salted water to cover in saucepan. Bring to boil on high heat, reduce to medium, place lid on, cook gently until soft.

Drain off water and dry potatoes, shaking off and on heat for a second.

Put potatoes, a few at a time, through ricer, being careful not to crush potatoes as you rice them. Add sprinkle of salt and pepper and lump of butter and serve at once.

Fluffy Whipped Potatoes

cooking time about 25 min

utensils
    saucepan with lid
    ricer
    wooden spoon
serves as many as you wish
    (4 for 4 servings)

4 medium-sized Idaho potatoes, peeled and cut in half
water to cover
½ tsp salt to put in water
4 tbsp butter, room temperature, to taste
½ cup milk or more if needed
salt and pepper to taste

Bring potatoes in salted water to boil, put lid on, reduce heat to medium. Cook 20-25 min until tender. Drain, shake pan over heat to dry. Do not burn.

Put potatoes through ricer; it makes fluffier potatoes than an electric mixer.

Heat milk until hot, add to potatoes, beating in with wooden spoon, add butter, beat until light. Add salt and pepper to taste. If necessary, add a little more hot milk or butter to have nice light whipped potatoes.

Scalloped Potatoes

cooking time 35-40 min
 preheat oven 425°

utensils
 shallow baking dish
serves 4

1 lb waxy boiling potatoes (about 3 cups), sliced thin, about ⅛ inch thick, put in cold water until needed
½ peeled clove garlic, halved (optional)
1 tbsp butter, room temperature, to smear baking dish
2 tbsp parmesan or swiss cheese, grated
1 tsp salt and pepper to taste
2 tbsp butter to dot potatoes
½ cup boiling milk

Rub baking dish with cut garlic, then butter.

Wipe potatoes dry, place half in rows in baking dish without overlapping, sprinkle with half the salt and pepper, dot with half the butter, then sprinkle half the cheese on. Repeat with the rest. Pour in the boiling milk. Bake 35-40 min until potatoes are tender, milk is absorbed and top is a beautiful brown.

can fix partially ahead

Fried Potato Balls

cooking time time to steam or boil; time to fry (5-10 min)

utensils
 steamer or saucepan
 skillet (teflon-lined is fine)
 tongs
serves as many as you wish

4-6 marble-sized potatoes per person, depending on appetite (16-24 for 4)
larger potatoes use smaller amount
butter or margarine to fry
salt and pepper to taste

Steam or boil marble-sized potatoes (see "Steaming" and "Tested Times for Steaming Vegetables"). Peel. Heat skillet with fat, just enough to keep potatoes from sticking, season potatoes with salt, fry to a golden brown, reducing heat as necessary. Remove to paper towels to absorb fat. Correct seasoning. Add pepper.

Potato Puffs

cooking time 40-45 min
   preheat oven 400°

utensils
   saucepan
   electric mixer or ricer
   baking sheet
makes about 30 puffs

5 large Idaho potatoes, peeled, cut in half,
   placed in water to hold until cooked
¾ tsp salt
2 eggs
¼ cup matzo or cracker meal
vegetable oil to grease hands

Boil potatoes as usual 20-25 min; beat cooked, dried potatoes in mixer or ricer until mashed, add eggs, matzo meal and salt to taste. Beat until fluffy.

Moisten palms with oil, roll the whipped potatoes into balls the size of walnuts. Makes about 30 balls.

Bake on teflon sheet or greased sheet about 20 min until brown.

These baked puffs may be frozen and can be baked as needed in 400° preheated oven for 7-8 min.

Oven-fried Potato Balls

cooking time time to steam or
   boil; time to bake (20-25
   min)
   preheat oven 450°

utensils
   steamer or saucepan
   pie plate or cake pan
   tongs
serves as many as you wish

ingredients as in "Fried Potato Balls" (see its recipe)

Dip steamed, peeled potatoes into melted fat, sprinkle with salt and pepper, place in pie plate, bake 20-25 min until browned in preheated 450° oven.

Potato Knishes

cooking time 20-30 min
   preheat oven 375°

utensils
   saucepan with lid
   skillet
   electric mixer or ricer
   baking sheet
makes about 26

*dough for "Never-fail Double Piecrust"
  (see its recipe)
3 large, mealy, Idaho potatoes, p e e l e d,
  placed in cold water
1 large onion, minced
3 tbsp vegetable shortening
salt and pepper to taste

Put dough in refrigerator until ready to use.

Boil potatoes in water until soft; meanwhile fry onion in vegetable shortening until soft but don't brown or burn. Dry potatoes by shaking over heat. Mash potatoes in mixer or ricer, stir in onions and shortening they were fried in. Add salt and pepper, set aside.

Follow exactly the "Beef Knishes" recipe, substituting potato mixture for beef mixture. Bake as directed in that recipe.

HANDY GRATER. The easiest way to grate raw potatoes or onions.

Potato Cakes

cooking time time to fry

utensils
   mixing bowl
   grater
   skillet
serves 4

3 large Idaho potatoes, peeled, placed in
   cold water
1 tbsp flour
1 egg stirred with fork
½ tsp salt to taste
vegetable shortening, enough to fill skillet
   ¼ inch deep

Immediately before frying, wipe potatoes one at a time,
grate into bowl. Mix in the salt, flour and egg.

Preheat heavy skillet with shortening on high heat. Drop
as many spoonfuls of potato cake mixture as skillet
will hold without crowding, being sure that you
will be able to turn them easily. Reduce heat to
medium, fry cakes on each side to a good brown,
drain on paper towels, keep hot in oven, serve as
soon as possible.

*Potato cakes are fine with brisket, duck or goose and taste well with
a sweet-sour apple sauce. These are wonderful to fry in a teflon skillet,
but don't use as much fat.*

can be prepared ahead

Sherried Sweet Potatoes

cooking time steam 30 min
bake 10-15 min
broil a few min

utensils
steamer or saucepan
shallow heatproof baking
dish
serves 4

2 medium-large steamed or boiled yams or
sweet potatoes
soft butter or mazola to smear baking dish
8 tbsp sherry
8 tbsp pineapple juice
4 tbsp brown sugar
4 tbsp softened butter

Steam potatoes as usual (See "Steaming" and "Tested
Times for Steaming Vegetables"), or boil them in
water to cover, which is just as good. Peel them and
cut into 1-inch slices, arrange in baking dish, don't
overlap. Stir sherry and pineapple juice together,
bring to boil, pour over potatoes. Bake uncovered
10-15 min in middle of oven. Sprinkle sugar on
potatoes, dot with butter, place under broiler to
melt and brown. Serve in individual dishes and be
sure to spoon the delicious sauce over the potatoes.

glazed with mandarin oranges; fix ahead

Hot Sweet Potato Pudding

cooking time about 20 min
preheat oven 375°

utensils
    mixing bowl
    food mill
    casserole
    small saucepan
serves 6

3 cups canned yams or sweet potatoes
½ tsp salt
½ cup honey
3 tbsp melted butter
½ tsp nutmeg
½ tsp ginger
¼ cup sherry
3 tbsp heavy cream
1 (11-oz) can mandarin oranges
1 tsp arrowroot or cornstarch

Drain yams; put through food mill.

Gradually combine all ingredients except oranges and
arrowroot with drained, mashed yams.

Butter the casserole, spoon the yam mixture in. Bake
20-30 min.

Drain oranges (there will be almost ½ cup juice). Mix
1 tbsp juice and 1 tsp arrowroot, add to rest of
juice, heat until juice becomes clear and has body.
Pour over oranges to glaze them. Arrange them
on the hot pudding and serve.

You can vary the pudding by omitting mandarin oranges
and alternating pudding in layers with strained
crushed canned pineapple, the top being potato
pudding.

can fix ahead

Steamed Rice

cooking time 15-20 min

utensils
    saucepan and lid
makes 3 cups

1 cup converted rice
2 cups water
1 tsp salt
1 small piece bay leaf
1 sprig parsley

Bring water with salt to boil, add bay leaf, parsley and rice, bring back to boil, turn heat to simmer, put lid on, simmer 18 min without looking, set off heat 10 min, remove lid, with fork cut through rice to fluff it up. Remove bay leaf and parsley and serve.

If you have to hold rice, either keep hot over hot water on very low heat, or place in oven at lowest heat with door open, or let get cold and reheat by shaking off and on heat, adding a spoon or so of hot water.

You can add butter to the rice for added flavor or heat in a little strong chicken broth.

you lose vitamins but gain flavor; can fix ahead and reheat

Rice--The French Method

cooking time about 12 min

utensils
    very large saucepot or kettle
    colander
serves 4-5

1 cup Carolina or other long grain or converted rice
8 quarts water
2 tbsp salt

Bring water and salt to a rapid boil. Gradually drop in rice without stopping boiling or bring back to rolling boil; boil 12 min. Taste a grain of rice to see if cooked to your liking.

Put rice in colander under running water. Return to saucepot, shake over heat to dry. Serve with butter or whatever you prefer or just as is. Each grain is separate and has a real rice flavor and no starch.

Never stir rice except with fork. One cup raw rice makes 3 cups cooked.

Risotto
--Baked in the Oven

cooking time about 35 min
preheat oven 375°

utensils
large skillet
fireproof glass casserole
with lid
saucepan
serves 4-5

1 cup converted rice
2 tbsp finely minced onion
4 tbsp butter
2 cups chicken broth
1 tsp salt
grind of pepper

Sauté onion in butter for about 5 min until soft, not brown. Blend in rice, stir over moderate heat 5 min until a light golden color, not brown. Boil broth with salt, pour slowly into casserole before adding sautéed onion and rice. Run fork through rice. Put lid on, place on third shelf from bottom, bake 5 min until simmering, reduce heat to 350°, bake 18 min with lid on. Check to see if broth has evaporated, if not, bake a few more min, test again by removing lid and tasting a grain of rice. If tender, remove from oven, run fork through rice 4 or 5 times to fluff and keep from sticking to bottom. The rice should be bitey. If you prefer it softer, put lid back on, leave out of oven 15-20 min to soften.

If rice has to be kept, turn heat to very lowest, or turn it off. Keep door open, put lid on rice and keep.

very flavorful

Risotto
--Cooked in Chicken Broth

cooking time 25 min

utensils
  saucepan
  wooden spoon
  2 forks
serves 4-5

1½ tsp butter or margarine
1 cup long grain converted rice
⅛ cup dry white wine or vermouth
¼ tsp salt to taste
about 2¼ cups boiling chicken broth
2 tbsp minced parsley (optional)

Melt butter, stir in rice without washing, reduce heat to low, stir about 5 min until rice looks creamy. Add wine, cook until absorbed, add boiling broth to cover rice, put lid on. Continue cooking on low until broth is absorbed, add more boiling broth, continue as before, correct seasoning, check whether rice is tender. If not, continue adding a little boiling broth, cook. Test until the broth is absorbed, and the rice is tender.

Each grain should be separate, not mushy. Run 2 forks through rice to fluff. Take off heat. Put cover on, and let it sit off heat 5 min before serving.

This can be varied by adding minced parsley or ½ cup grated parmesan cheese before you let it sit 5 min. You can also vary this by first sautéeing ¼ cup finely minced onion, just until it is soft, not browned, before stirring in the uncooked rice and continue as the above recipe says.

fresh or canned, a quickie

Deviled Wild Rice

cooking time just enough to heat

utensils
colander
heavy heatproof casserole
or saucepan
serves 4

1 cup wild rice, cooked as per instructions on pkg, or 1 (12-oz) can
1 (10-oz) can chicken broth
1 jar pepita nuts
½ cup dried onion flakes
2 chicken bouillon cubes
4 tbsp butter
pepper to taste

Run cold water over canned rice to freshen it, or use cooked wild rice, drain well. Combine all ingredients over high heat until most of liquid is absorbed. Correct seasoning.

129

Fresh Corn on the Cob

cooking time 5 min after coming to boil

utensils
very large saucepot or kettle
tongs
serves as many as you like

enough water to fill kettle or saucepot ¾ full
2 ears corn per person

We never serve corn on the cob except in season; we use frozen corn otherwise. I have a habit when buying corn to pay for 1 ear and taste it; if sweet, I buy as many as needed; otherwise I say, "Thank you," and go on my way.

Corn should be kept on ice until ready to use or in refrigerator to retain its sweetness. The best corn is from the corn patch to the kettle.

Remove husks as close to cooking time as possible.

Bring water to a rolling boil. Drop ears in one at a time until all have been added, bring water back to boil as quickly as possible. Boil 5 min. Remove with tongs. Serve with individual salt shakers and melted butter.

We usually serve our corn as a first course, to savor every bit of sweetness.

Soufflé Corn Pudding

cooking time 35 min
    preheat oven 325°

utensils
    mixing bowl
    rotary beater
    baking dish (casserole)
serves **4**

1 (1-lb 1-oz) can creamed corn
½ cup milk
salt and pepper to taste
¼ tsp nutmeg
2 tbsp melted butter
3 egg yolks
3 egg whites
softened butter or margarine to smear baking dish

Combine creamed corn, milk, seasoning, melted butter and egg yolks. Fold in stiffly beaten egg whites. Spoon into casserole. Bake 35 min. Serve at once; it can't wait.

a simple gourmet dish

Deep South Yellow Grits

cooking time 15 min

utensils
    saucepan
    wooden spoon
serves **4**

1 cup yellow grits
3 cups cold water
1 tsp salt to taste
2 tbsp butter or more to taste

Add grits to water and salt, bring to boil. Reduce to simmer, stir, cook, add butter until thick and luscious.

Always use cold water with grits to start them. This is the old-fashioned way, and it hasn't been improved on, as it insures no lumps.

Corn Fritters

cooking time 10-15 min

utensils
    mixing bowls
    sifter
    skillet
    rotary beater
serves 4 small eaters, 2 big
    eaters

1 cup canned cream corn
2 large eggs, yolks separated from whites
½ tsp salt
grind of pepper to taste
1 cup all-purpose flour
1 tsp double-action baking powder
vegetable shortening to make ½ inch fat
    in skillet

Mix together creamed corn, egg yolks, flour either sifted or mixed with baking powder, salt, pepper, to make a thick batter.

Beat whites stiff but not dry, so that they will form peaks when you lift beaters; fold into batter.

Heat fat until hot, test by dropping small piece of bread; if it rises at once, starts browning, the fat is ready. Drop batter by spoonfuls, being careful not to crowd, so they will have room to puff up and brown quickly.

For a second, drain on paper towels placed on rack to circulate air. This keeps them from getting soggy; serve at once.

fix ahead, finish later

Zucchini, Pattypan Squash or Eggplant in Wine Sauce

cooking time steaming or boiling time + 10-15 min baking time
preheat oven 350°

utensils
steamer or saucepan to boil vegetables
saucepan for mixing sauce
casserole
serves 4

4 medium-size unpeeled squash or 2 small eggplants
1 large or 2 (8-oz) cans Arturo sauce or marinara sauce
3 tbsp sauterne or sherry
pinch of salt
topping of French-fried onions, canned or grated parmesan cheese, or buttered or plain crumbs

Wash vegetables, wipe dry, cut into large cubes and steam or boil (see "Steaming," "Tested Times for Steaming Vegetables," and "Tested Times for Boiling Fresh Vegetables").

Stir wine into sauce before combining with steamed or boiled vegetable. Set aside until ready to use. Top with one of the toppings listed, heat in oven 10-15 min.

You can make another sauce with 1 (8-oz) can stewed tomatoes, cooked 5 min with 3 drops tabasco sauce and 1 tbsp sauterne, thickened with 2 tiny butter balls made of ½ tsp butter mixed with ½ tsp flour. Combine sauce with squash and heat in oven 10-15 min, top with one of toppings for a different taste.

Baked Pattypan Squash

cooking time about 15-20 min
preheat oven 350°

utensils
  skillet
  casserole or baking dish
serves 4

1 unpeeled pattypan or zucchini squash or
  eggplant
½ cup fresh onions, minced
4 allspice or ¼ tsp ground allspice
1 (1-lb) can tomatoes
½ tsp salt to taste
1 garlic clove
pinch of sugar
margarine to fry, as needed

Wash vegetable, wipe dry and cut into ¼-inch thick slices.

Fry vegetable on medium heat until browned. Remove to paper-covered plate to drain off fat. Wipe out skillet, replace margarine, soften onions, but don't brown. Combine the tomatoes and rest of ingredients, stir, cook until liquid has evaporated and sauce is thick. Remove garlic and whole allspice.

Arrange the browned vegetable in casserole, pour sauce over, bake 10 min until hot.

134

Fried Pattypan Squash or Eggplant

cooking time 5-10 min

utensils
  mixing bowl
  skillet
serves 4

4 small unpeeled pattypan squash or 1-2
  young small unpeeled eggplants
1 cup flour, seasoned with ¼ tsp salt, as
  needed
1 large egg, stirred with fork
2 tbsp milk
vegetable shortening as needed
tiny bit of butter added for flavor

Wash, dry and slice vegetables thinly.

Preheat skillet, dip the squash or eggplant into egg
  mixed with milk, then into flour, lightly but coating
  it all over, sauté. Do not crowd them in skillet.
  Brown each side a lovely golden brown, place on
  heated platter to serve.

These should be crisp and have a fresh taste.

fix ahead, bake later

Baked Acorn Squash

cooking time 25-30 min
  preheat oven 400°

utensils
  shallow baking dish with
    lid
serves 4

2 acorn squash
4 tsp butter
½ tsp salt
4 tsp brown sugar or honey
4 tsp sherry or bourbon
sprinkle of nutmeg for each half
butter to smear baking dish

Wash squash, wipe dry, cut in halves and remove seeds.

Smear butter inside squash, season with salt, brown
  sugar, sherry or bourbon, a little sprinkle of nutmeg. Bake until tender about 25-30 min.

fix ahead

Sautéed Mushrooms

cooking time about 10 min

utensils
  skillet
serves 2-4

½ lb fresh mushrooms
3 tbsp butter or margarine
salt to taste

If necessary, wash mushrooms, wipe dry or just wipe with damp paper towels before cutting off dried-out brown end of stem. The mushrooms can be sautéed whole or cut in half, lengthwise, through caps and stems or into slices the same way.

When butter is hot, add mushrooms, sauté 4-5 min, shaking pan off and on heat to brown, not burn, mushrooms. Season to taste.

Mushrooms may be cooked earlier, as they reheat without loss of flavor.

these stay white

Cooked White Mushrooms

cooking time about 5 min

utensils
  teflon or enameled sauce-
            pan
serves 2-4

½ lb fresh mushrooms
¾ cup water
¼ tsp salt
1 tbsp lemon juice, strained
1 tbsp butter

Trim and wash mushrooms as in above recipe, cut as you wish.

Bring ingredients to boil before adding mushrooms. Shake saucepan, so mushrooms are covered with liquid, cover, boil 5 min on medium heat. Set aside until needed.

The lemon keeps the mushrooms white.

136

a quickie, fix ahead

Steamed Onions

cooking time about 25 min

utensils
    steamer
    teflon skillet
serves 4

16 little white onions
2 tbsp butter
salt and pepper to taste
4 cups water to steam onions

Peel onions, cut off stems under running water to keep from crying, being careful not to cut too close.

Steam onions (see "Steaming") about 20 min, run cold water to stop their cooking. Dry on paper towels, don't break skins.

Sauté in butter on medium heat until onions turn a lovely brown, add salt and pepper to taste. These onions are so sweet, they don't need added sugar. Serve with meat or turkey.

If you are in a hurry, use tiny canned onions, first running cold water over them to help remove the canned taste. Wipe carefully and brown just as you do the fresh ones. Season well.

Braised Fresh Onions

cooking time 20 min

utensils
  steamer
  skillet
serves 4

*16 small white onions, steamed (see "Steaming")
*1 pkg Knorr's dehydrated chicken noodle soup mixed with 2 cups water
2 tbsp butter
pinch of thyme
very small ¼ piece of bay leaf
1 sprig parsley
salt and pepper to taste

Steam white onions 15 min. In meantime make chicken soup by bringing water and dehydrated soup to boil, reduce heat, cook 10 min, strain, use ¼ cup only, set rest aside to use another time.

Sauté onions in butter until brown, add soup with herb seasoning, braise 5 min. Correct seasoning, remove parsley and bay leaf, serve hot.

You can use canned onions, freshening them with cold water to remove canned taste, and follow the recipe above.

Creamed White Onions

cooking time about 25 min

utensils
  steamer
  skillet
  saucepan
serves 4

*16 onions, steamed and sautéed as in immediately preceding recipe (see "Steaming")
1 tbsp butter
1 tbsp flour
½ cup milk
½ cup cream
salt and pepper to taste

Melt butter, off heat stir in flour, then milk and cream, bring to boil, reduce heat, cook about 5 min. Add salt and pepper to taste, pour over sautéed onions, heat thoroughly and serve.

You can substitute canned onions for fresh.

Glazed Steamed Carrots

cooking time about 15 min

utensils
  steamer and saucepot
  skillet
serves 4

12-15 whole, young, thin carrots, peeled
⅛ tsp salt
4 tbsp honey or sugar
4 tbsp butter

Steam carrots (see "Steaming") as follows: bring 4 cups water to boil in saucepot. Place steamer in before adding carrots, put lid on, boil until steam appears. Reduce heat to medium-high; steam about 15 min. Taste to see that carrots are firm but done as you like them.

Remove carrots to skillet heated with butter and honey or sugar and salt. Glaze by rolling the carrots around in mixture on medium heat until glazed, about 4-5 min.

easy; fix ahead

Baked Beans

cooking time about 15 min

utensils
    casserole or saucepan
    casserole to serve in
serves 2

1 (1-lb) can Heinz's vegetarian beans
½ cup vegetable juice
1 tsp Gulden's spicy brown mustard
¼ tsp dry mustard
⅛ tsp garlic powder
⅛ tsp onion powder
2 tsp sweet pickle juice
⅛ tsp tabasco
½ tsp Worcestershire sauce
4 pieces bacon, broiled, broken into pieces
tiny spicy sausages

Mix all the ingredients together except bacon, bring to a boil, reduce heat, simmer either on top of stove or in 375° oven 15 min, adding bacon to top of casserole the last 5 min.

good boiled in water, not steamed

Fresh Lima Beans

cooking time 15-20 min

utensils
    saucepan with lid
serves **4**

1-qt box shelled, green, fresh full lima beans
water to cover
½ tsp salt to taste
2 tbsp butter or margarine

Bring water, salt, butter to boil, add lima beans, bring back to boil, cover. Reduce heat to medium, boil gently about 15 min. Taste and test for doneness. Correct seasoning.

fix ahead

Green Beans and Almonds

cooking time 15 min for whole beans; 10 min for sliced beans

utensils
steamer or saucepan
serves 6-8

2 lb fresh or frozen green beans
1 cup almonds, in slivers
2-4 tbsp butter
salt to taste
grind of pepper

If using fresh beans, choose bright green, crisp, small green beans. Snap off ends or slice beans on the bias.

Steam beans according to instructions in "Steaming," "Tested Times for Steaming Vegetables," and "Tested Times for Steaming Frozen Vegetables."

You can prepare the beans earlier by running cold water over them to stop the cooking. You will preserve the nice green color. Set aside until ready to use.

Brown almonds a golden color, add to the green beans, toss over heat, correct seasoning, serve hot.

Broiled Tomatoes

cooking time about 7 min
   preheat broiler

utensils
   shallow roasting pan
serves **4**

2-3 large firm tomatoes
¼ cup seasoned bread crumbs
1 tbsp butter or margarine
1 tsp sugar
salt and pepper to taste

Slice tomatoes into ¾- or 1-inch slices, salt and pepper to taste, sprinkle sugar over before placing in buttered pan, sprinkle crumbs on slices and dot with butter. Broil on first shelf from heat until crusty brown, lower if necessary to cook.

The entire broiling time takes about 7 min.

fix ahead

Stuffed Baked Tomatoes

cooking time 10-15 min
   preheat oven 400°

utensils
   mixing bowl
   tin with sides to fit tomatoes
serves **4**

4 firm medium-sized or large tomatoes
½ cup seasoned crumbs
2 small cloves garlic, crushed, or ½ tsp dried garlic powder
2 tbsp onion, finely minced
salt and pepper to taste
2 tsp sugar
butter to smear pan
2 tsp butter to dot the crumbs on tomatoes

You can substitute Kellogg's croutettes rolled into crumbs or plain crumbs for seasoned crumbs by adding 2 tbsp minced fresh parsley, ½ tsp dry thyme.

Mix seasoned crumbs with crushed garlic, minced onion, salt and pepper to taste, set aside.

Wash and wipe tomatoes, remove stems, cut in half, sprinkle sugar, salt and pepper on lightly, before spooning on the seasoned crumbs. Place in tin, dot with butter, place in middle of oven, bake 10-15 min. Check at 10 min. The tomatoes may be baked.

You can vary this by scooping out the seeds from the tomatoes and stuffing with bread crumb mixture, proceeding as above.

143

Mashed Buttered Turnips

cooking time about 10 min

utensils
    steamer or saucepan
    ricer
serves **4**

12 small white turnips, peeled, quartered
2-4 tbsp butter
salt and pepper to taste

Steam turnips until tender (see "Steaming"), which takes about 10 min. Turnips are very watery and their texture is not smooth like potatoes.

Put turnips through ricer, being careful as you push down to push out water in turnips, which you can discard; then mash turnips, add butter, salt and pepper to taste.

Young white turnips are tasty enough without adding any sugar, the larger ones may need a pinch of sugar, but why buy old turnips in the first place?

Glazed Turnips

cooking time 10-15 min

utensils
    steamer or saucepan
    skillet
serves **4**

6 small white turnips, peeled and sliced
1 tbsp butter
1 tbsp sugar
½ cup Knorr's dehydrated onion soup
good sprinkle of nutmeg and ginger
salt and pepper to taste

Make soup as directed on pkg but use only 2 cups water; strain.

Steam sliced turnips 5-10 min (see "Steaming"), taste to test when tender, don't overcook. You can substitute a saucepan and boil turnips if you have no steamer.

Melt butter, stir in sugar, add turnips, cook 1 min, don't burn, shake skillet, add heated onion soup, nutmeg, ginger, and cook, stir until turnips are glazed. Correct seasoning.

Creamed Vegetables

cooking time 30 min
preheat oven 350°

utensils
  steamer
  casserole
  saucepan
serves 4

*4 cups steamed vegetables, your choice
(see "Steaming" and "Tested Times
for Steaming Vegetables")
2 cups thick cream
4 tbsp softened butter
salt and pepper to taste
butter to grease casserole

Select one, all, or as many as you like of these vegetables: cauliflower, broccoli, brussels sprouts, string beans, peas or carrots. We use any leftover vegetables or steam the ones we wish to use, running cold water to stop the cooking.

Smear butter in casserole before adding vegetables and butter, place in middle rack of oven, heat 10 min. While heating, bring cream to boil, pour over vegetables, mix lightly, return to oven, bake 10 min. Correct seasoning.

fix partially ahead

Cheesed Vegetables in Casserole

cooking time steaming time +
15 min baking time
preheat oven 350°

utensils
  steamer or saucepan
  casserole
serves 4

*4 cups steamed broccoli, asparagus, cauliflower or brussels sprouts (see "Steaming" and "Tested Times for Steaming Vegetables")
1 tbsp butter to smear casserole
½ cup grated cheddar cheese
½ cup grated parmesan cheese
2 tbsp melted butter

Steam vegetables.

Heat steamed vegetables, covered in oven 5 min, then mix in cheddar cheese, top with parmesan and pour melted butter over it. Bake uncovered about 10 min until the cheese is browned.

145

oil and vinegar

French Dressing

utensils
  salad bowl
serves 4

6 tbsp fresh oil (olive oil or your favorite)
2 tbsp mild wine vinegar
salt to taste
grind of pepper to taste

Pour oil over greens, toss so that all leaves are coated, then add wine vinegar and salt, toss without crushing tender greens, correct seasoning, grind pepper on to your taste.

Your salad will taste as good as the wine vinegar is. American wine vinegars are usually too strong, so taste and test to get a good one that you can continue to buy. If you live in a large city, try to get a French or an Italian wine vinegar. Spice Island, Pierce, and Monarch are good wine vinegars, and I'm sure there are others.

Blue Cheese Dressing

utensils
  screw-top jar
serves 4

2 heaping tbsp blue cheese dressing, to your taste

Mix greens with "Screw-Top Jar Salad Dressing" (see its recipe), lightly toss in the blue cheese dressing until thoroughly combined but don't crush greens —easy but tasty.

146

shake and make

Screw-Top Jar Salad Dressing

utensils
  screw-top jar
serves 4

6 tbsp fresh oil (olive oil or your favorite)
2 tbsp wine vinegar
½ clove garlic
⅛ tsp salt

Shake ingredients in small jar. Taste to correct seasoning. Let stand 15 min to season. Shake again, pour
over greens, add grind of pepper. Toss gently.

The secret of a good dressing is fresh oil. Buy your
favorite oil at a supermarket that sells a lot. Also,
if your family is small, buy small bottles. Wine
vinegar should be mild, not sharp. Most American
wine vinegars are too sharp, and the French and
Italian ones are hard to come by. Hunt around
for a good one. Lemon juice can be used as a
change from the vinegar.

Russian Dressing

utensils
  small mixing bowl
makes ½ cup

½ cup unsweetened mayonnaise
4 tbsp chili sauce
1 tbsp ketchup
2 tbsp lemon juice

Mix until smooth.

Good with shrimp as well as over vegetables.

Vinaigrette Sauce

utensils
  screw-top jar
makes about ½ cup

9 tbsp oil (olive or your favorite)
3 tbsp wine vinegar
½ tsp dried mustard
½ tsp dried chervil, 1 tsp dried tarragon, and ½ tsp dried basil, each steeped separately in ¼ cup boiling water, drained
1 tbsp finely minced scallions
1 tbsp finely minced fresh parsley
½ tsp salt to taste
grind of pepper

Shake all ingredients together in screw-top jar. Pour over whatever needs this sauce.

You can vary this sauce by adding 1 tbsp capers and ½ tsp of the caper broth to taste, using only the fresh herbs, such as parsley, scallions or chives.

This sauce is good with fish, cold beef and sliced tomatoes.

in the summertime only when you can get local homegrown tomatoes!

Sliced Tomatoes with Vinaigrette Sauce

utensils
  bowl or screw-top jar
serves as many as you wish

luscious ripe but firm tomatoes, not mealy
  ones
*"Vinaigrette Sauce" (see its recipe)
parsley, minced fine

Slice tomatoes into luscious medium slices just before dinner. Place on platter, pour vinaigrette sauce over them, sprinkle chopped fresh parsley and enjoy your summer's simple pleasure.

Cucumber Salad

utensils
  mixing bowl
serves 4

3 cucumbers, peeled and sliced thin
½ Bermuda or regular medium onion,
  sliced very thin, or scallions
3 tbsp sugar
¼ cup sour cream
¼ cup vinegar
½ cup cold water
1 tsp salt
pepper

Mix vinegar, sugar and water together. Sprinkle salt over cucumbers and onion before pouring vinegar mixture on them, marinate 30 min in refrigerator.

When ready to serve, drain off liquid and stir in sour cream and, last, a good grind of pepper.

This is a good salad with fish and cold meats. It can also be served without the sour cream and just a sprinkle of pepper.

149

Tossed Green Salad

utensils
large bowl big enough to
   toss the greens without
   crushing or bruising
garlic press
serves **4**

Boston lettuce
bibb lettuce
romaine lettuce
iceberg lettuce
escarole
chicory
endive
watercress
1 clove garlic
scallions (1 stalk minced fine, greens and
   bulb put into wax bag in refrigerator
   until needed)
9 tbsp oil (olive or your favorite)
3 tbsp mild wine vinegar
salt to taste
good grind of pepper

Either rub bowl with cut garlic or put unpeeled garlic
(unpeeled so it will be easy to remove from press)
in garlic press, and press over the greens after you
have put them into bowl. Place greens in gently,
cutting with sharp knife those that are too big. I
am not of the "tear the greens" school, as that
crushes the greens.

The proportion of oil to vinegar is 3 tbsp oil to 1 tbsp
wine vinegar; the greens glisten from the oil. You
can decrease or increase the wine vinegar to suit
your individual taste.

There are two ways to prepare the dressing, both very
easy. One is to pour oil over greens and toss, then
add wine vinegar, adding salt and pepper last. The
other method is to shake oil and vinegar together
in jar until they become cloudy or creamy-looking,
pour over greens, adding salt and pepper to taste.

In either method add a little salt to taste so you can
add more if necessary and not oversalt. Add dressing in both methods at the last minute, including a
grind of pepper just before sending to the table.

This salad is so simple, it complements all kinds of meat and chicken. You can vary it by adding some dry mustard, about ¼ tsp, to the oil and vinegar, or wet mustard or you can add fresh herbs, when you can get them, such as chives, chervil, tarragon, and the always available parsley. If you wish, you can freshen dried herbs by steeping them in boiling water 15 min. We love to add thin-sliced cucumbers or chunks of cucumbers, and sometimes thin-sliced crisp rosy red radishes and cut cubes of tomatoes, which we place at the bottom of the bowl before putting in the greens. Since the cherry tomatoes are available out of season and are better at such times than the large ones, slice them in half and use.

Many times escarole greens are bitter, and for those of you who prefer them not bitter, do this: place them 2 min in hot water, remove to warm water 5 min and cold water 7 min. Refrigerate.

Cole Slaw

utensils
large mixing bowl
grater
makes about 2 cups

2 cups shredded cabbage, cut fine with knife or 1 small green cabbage, shredded
1 carrot, grated fine
¼ cup vinegar to taste
2 tsp sugar to taste
3 tsp unsweetened mayonnaise
salt and pepper to taste

Mix mayonnaise, vinegar and sugar together. Pour over cabbage and carrot, toss lightly, add salt and pepper to taste and serve at once. Cole slaw doesn't improve with standing, as it gets watery and loses some flavor.

Belgian Endive Salad

utensils
   screw-top jar to make
     vinaigrette sauce
   glass pie plate
serves 4

6 Belgian endives
3 hard-boiled eggs, minced
1 (8-oz) can pickled beets, cut into
   julienne strips
*double portion "Vinaigrette Sauce" (see its
   recipe)

Wash endives thoroughly, cut off dried stumps, halve lengthwise.

Make vinaigrette sauce, set aside. Put endives in pie plate, pour some of the vinaigrette souce over them, let marinate in refrigerator about 1 hr. When ready to use, put on individual salad plates, arrange beets on top, decorate with chopped eggs. Pour remaining dressing over salad, add grind of pepper.

appetizer on a hot day

Stuffed Tomatoes

cooking time 5 min
utensils
   skillet
serves 4

4 medium tomatoes
4 eggs
salt and pepper
4 small bulbs scallions, minced fine
parsley or watercress

Scoop out insides of tomatoes, season with salt and pepper, turn upside down to drain.

Scramble eggs, let cool. Mix with minced scallions. Stuff tomatoes, place them on bed of parsley or watercress.

This looks pretty and tastes good.

152

Quickie Pickled Beets

utensils
bowl
serves 2

1 (8-oz.) can tiny sweet beets (Libby's is good)
4 whole allspice
2 bay leaves
3 tbsp white vinegar
1 very small onion, peeled and sliced thin
sugar and salt to taste

Pour beets and beet juice into small bowl with sliced onion, pour vinegar over them, add bay leaves, allspice, sugar and salt to taste. Place in refrigerator to season. Correct seasoning.

Gourmet Sauerkraut

Most canned sauerkrauts have a very ordinary taste. White wine added will improve the flavor.

Add 1/3 cup sauterne, or other white wine that isn't dry, to an 8-oz can of sauerkraut. Toss together in bowl, using 2 forks; do not push down.

Marinate in a jar in the refrigerator overnight. It will keep in refrigerator about 2 weeks.

This kraut can be heated and served with pork or sausage; a few dried juniper berries also add a nice touch, if you have them.

The good German cooks always add wine when cooking their sauerkraut with their delicious German sausage.

153

Marie's Bean Salad

utensils
  chopper
  bowl
makes about 3 cups

3 hard-boiled eggs, minced
2 cans Great Northern beans, strained
    under running cold water
½ cup onion, minced fine
¼ cup celery, minced fine
8 Heinz's gherkins, quartered and sliced
½ cup unsweetened mayonnaise, diluted
    with 2 tbsp milk
salt and pepper to taste

Mix all ingredients together gently but thoroughly, being
    careful not to mash beans. Correct seasoning. Place
    in refrigerator to season.

String Bean Salad

utensils
  2 bowls
makes about 5 cups

4 cups cooked or canned firm string beans,
    cut into 1¼-inch pieces
¼ cup green pepper, minced fine
¼ cup celery, minced fine
¼ cup scallions, minced fine
¼ cup onions, minced fine
¼ cup pecans, cut into pieces
6 tbsp strained lemon juice
1 tbsp white vinegar
2 tsp sugar
½ cup Miracle Whip dressing
1 tbsp sour cream
salt to taste
⅛ tsp pepper

Mix Miracle Whip with vinegar, sugar, sour cream and
    lemon juice until smooth.

Combine rest of ingredients, then pour sauce over and
    mix until well blended.

Kidney Bean Salad

utensils
   bowl
   colander
makes about 2 cups

1 can firm kidney beans
2 eggs, hard-boiled and diced
¼ cup celery, minced
¼ cup onion, minced
¼ cup unsweetened mayonnaise
¼ tsp salt to taste
good grind of pepper (about ⅛ tsp)

Take out 2 tbsp bean broth from can and set aside. Run cold water over beans in colander.

Combine all ingredients, including bean broth, being careful not to crush beans. Place in refrigerator to season.

fix ahead

Marinated String Bean Salad

utensils
   bowl
   screw-top jar
makes about 2 cups

1 can firm small whole string beans (such as Blue Lake), strained

VINAIGRETTE SAUCE
½ cup oil
2 tbsp wine vinegar
½ tsp dried mustard mixed with a little of the wine vinegar
1 tbsp finely chopped scallions
¼ tsp salt to taste
pepper to taste
½ tsp dried chervil (optional)
1 tbsp dried tarragon
1 tbsp finely minced fresh parsley
½ tsp dried basil (optional)

Shake the sauce in screw-top jar and pour over beans, marinate, turning once in a while until the beans are tasty.

Asparagus Salad

utensils
    pie plate to marinate salad
serves 4

2 (13-oz) jars firm large green asparagus
⅓ cup white distilled vinegar
3 tsp sugar
½ cup vegetable oil
1 cucumber, sliced thin
1 green pepper, sliced very thin into rings
½ tsp salt to taste
grind of pepper

Mix sugar, vinegar, oil and salt, pour over asparagus arranged in pie plate. Marinate 5-6 hr in refrigerator. Before serving, place asparagus on salad plates, arrange cucumbers and thin slices of pepper on top, pour some of the marinating juice on, add grind of pepper.

This is also very good served with a "dollop" of "Brandy Sauce" (see its recipe) or "Easy Home-made Mayonnaise" (see its recipe). It also is enhanced by "Oilless Vinaigrette Sauce with Mayonnaise," first variation (see its recipe).

fix ahead

Grapefruit Salad

utensils
  sharp paring knife
  mixing jar
serves 4

3 large sweet grapefruit, segments cut out
chickory, golden inner leaves, washed, crisped in refrigerator
watercress
FRENCH DRESSING
9-12 tbsp oil
juice from grapefruit
¼ tsp paprika
¼ tsp dried garlic powder or clove of fresh garlic
salt and pepper to taste

Cut the peeling and the white pulp off grapefruit, then cut segments out, using sharp pointed knife. Be sure to save all the juice to use in the dressing.

Shake all dressing ingredients together in jar until well mixed and cloudy; correct seasoning. If grapefruit are very sour, add ¼ tsp sugar to dressing.

Arrange grapefruit segments on beds of chicory and watercress and pour salad dressing over them.

157

Lynda's Salad

utensils
    individual salad plates
serves **4**

1 sweet cantaloupe, Persian or honeydew
    melon cut into half-moon slices
2 large cold ripe tomatoes cut into 8 slices
    right before serving

Arrange slices of cantaloupe on one side of the individual salad plates and slices of tomato on the other so that they look appetizing.

Serve "Lynda's Tart Lemony Dressing" with it (see its recipe).

This salad is a nice contrast in texture and taste.

fix ahead

Carrot-Pineapple Mold

utensils
    mixing bowl
    mold
serves **4**

1 cup crushed, canned pineapple
juice of 1 lemon, strained
cold water
1 carrot, grated
1 cup boiling water
1 box lemon or orange jello

Strain pineapple; set juice aside.

Add enough cold water to lemon juice and pineapple juice to make 1 cup liquid.

Stir boiling water into jello until it dissolves.

Add lemon juice mixture to hot jello, then crushed pineapple and grated carrot.

Run cold water over the mold, pour in jello mixture, place in refrigerator to jell.

To unmold, dip mold quickly in hot water a few times for a second, turn out onto a serving plate.

This can be made in individual molds as well.

Lynda's Tart Lemony Dressing

utensils
   mixing bowl
   garlic press
   spoon
serves 4

½ clove garlic, crushed
8 oz Miracle Whip dressing
6 tbsp strained lemon juice
1 tbsp wine vinegar or distilled vinegar
¼ tsp paprika

Gradually stir paprika into Miracle Whip until smooth,
then stir in rest of ingredients.

This is a very good dressing to serve with seafood or a vegetable salad.

fix ahead

Strawberry Jello Mold

utensils
   strainer
   mixing bowl
   mold

2 pkg frozen strawberries, sweetened
about 1⅔ cups canned, crushed pineapple
1 pkg Knox gelatin
2 pkg strawberry jello
2 cups boiling water
2 small bananas
½ pint sour cream

Defrost strawberries, strain, set juice aside.

Strain crushed pineapple, set juice aside. Add pineapple juice to strawberry juice. Add crushed pineapple to strawberries.

Mix pineapple and strawberry juice with gelatin. Add
jello, stir in boiling water. Stir in strawberry and
pineapple mixture.

Mash bananas, add to strawberry mixture. Put half in
mold. Place in refrigerator. When it is firm, spread
sour cream over it. Pour remaining strawberry mixture on top. Set in refrigerator to harden. When
hardened, turn over and place hot towel on the bottom of the mold to loosen. Turn out on plate.

This keeps very well and may be made the day before.

fix ahead; a perfect meal for a hot day

Mediterranean Salad

utensils
large platter
serves 6

*4-5 cups "Pennsylvania Dutch Potato Salad" (see its recipe), or sliced potatoes marinated in *"Vinaigrette Sauce" (see its recipe)
*8 "Stuffed Eggs" (see its recipe)
*"Marinated String Bean Salad" (see its recipe)
2 hard-boiled egg whites, diced and sprinkled over string beans just before arranging salad
3 (7-oz) cans tuna fish
1 large head Boston lettuce
2 pt boxes cherry tomatoes or 4 large firm tomatoes, peeled and sliced
2-3 (1¼-oz) cans anchovy filets
1 (8-oz) jar black olives
1 green pepper, cut into rings
¼ cup capers
4 lemons, quartered
¼ cup parsley, chopped fine
1 pt mayonnaise, Hellman's unsweetened or *"Easy Homemade Mayonnaise" (see its recipe)
salt and pepper to taste

Either place a glass bowl containing the mayonnaise, if homemade, in center of platter, or the potato salad without the bowl, if using a bought mayonnaise, which you place elsewhere on the platter.

Arrange each food attractively in lettuce leaves, accenting with capers, anchovy filets, chopped hard-boiled whites on string beans, black olives, and parsley. When all are arranged attractively, sprinkle chopped parsley over as a finishing touch.

160

Macaroni Salad

utensils
   large kettle
   mixing bowl
   wire strainer
   colander
serves 4-6

MACARONI
1 (8-oz) box elbow macaroni, firm type
3 qt water
1 tbsp salt

SALAD
4 hard-boiled eggs, whites minced, yolks pushed through strainer
¼ cup distilled white vinegar
2 tbsp sugar
2 tbsp French's prepared mustard
½ green pepper, minced
¼ cup celery, minced
¼ cup onion, minced
1 tsp celery seed
1 tsp salt to taste
¼ tsp pepper to taste
½ cup unsweetened mayonnaise

To cook macaroni, boil water and salt, gradually add macaroni, cook 9-12 min according to tenderness desired; stir occasionally so it doesn't stick, don't over-cook. Drain in colander, run cold water over to cool macaroni as quickly as possible, set aside.

Stir hard-boiled egg yolks into vinegar and mix with sugar and mustard.

Combine all ingredients except mayonnaise with macaroni in bowl, then stir it in very gently. Correct seasoning. Place in refrigerator to season.

Pennsylvania Dutch Potato Salad

utensils
wire strainer
mixing bowl
small bowl
makes 4-5 cups

4 cups, peeled, cubed waxy potatoes, put in cold water
2 tsp salt to taste
¼ cup distilled vinegar mixed with 1½ tbsp sugar
2 hard-boiled eggs, separated, whites minced and yolks pushed through strainer into bowl
½ cup unsweetened mayonnaise gradually stirred into sieved yolks
½ cup celery, minced fine
½ cup onion, minced fine
¼ tsp celery seed
pepper to taste

Bring the potatoes to boil, add 1 tsp salt. Reduce heat to medium, put lid on, boil gently about 4 min or until tender but firm. Drain. Place in large bowl, pour vinegar mixture on, let cool. Add rest of ingredients, being careful not to mash potatoes. Mixing with your hands is the best way. Add pepper, correct seasoning, place in refrigerator.

fix ahead; good for a ladies' luncheon and good for a man anytime

Seafood Mediterranean Salad

utensils
platter
2 forks
serves 4-6

*3 cups "Steamed Rice" (see its recipe)
½ cup vegetable oil
8 tbsp tarragon vinegar
salt and pepper to taste, for rice
12 green stuffed olives, sliced
½ sweet green pepper, sliced thin
*"Vinaigrette Sauce" (see its recipe)
3 large firm tomatoes sliced to form base for salad
*2 lb "Steamed Shrimp" (see its recipe)
1 can lump crab meat
¼ cup or more parsley, minced

With two forks mix oil into rice, set aside tomatoes, vinaigrette sauce and minced parsley. Add rest of ingredients to rice, season with tarragon vinegar, being careful not to crush crab meat, correct seasoning. In place of tarragon vinegar, you can use white vinegar by adding to it 2 tsp dried tarragon steeped in ¼ cup boiling water 15 min and strained.

Place tomatoes seasoned with vinaigrette sauce on individual plates, add seafood salad, decorate with minced parsley.

fix ahead

Canned Salmon
with Vinegar and Onion

serves 2

1 (7-oz) can salmon
⅓ cup onion, minced fine
4 tbsp vinegar to taste

Sprinkle onion and vinegar over salmon, serve with some slices of tomato and some crusty bread.

This is a very simple dish but is very tasty for lunch, especially on a hot day.

163

Shrimp and Baby Lobster Tails Salad

cooking time 6 min to steam shrimp and lobster

utensils
saucepan
platter
serves 4-8

*2 lb "Steamed Shrimp" (see its recipe)
*2 lb baby lobster tails, steamed, peeled and deveined (see "Steamed Langostinas or Baby Lobster Tails")
2 cucumbers peeled, sliced thin, marinated in oil and vinegar dressing
2 bunches or 2 pkg small whole bright red radishes, crisp and ice cold
4 hearts of celery, halved
6 hard-boiled eggs, halved, sprinkled with minced parsley
*"Marinated String Bean Salad" (see its recipe)
1 (1-pt) box little cherry tomatoes, stuffed with anchovies

MAYONNAISE

2 cups Hellman's mayonnaise (the un-sweetened kind)
4 tsp ketchup
20 drops tabasco
8 tsp lemon juice
8 tsp lime juice
8 tsp pickle juice from Heinz's gherkins

Stir all the mayonnaise ingredients into mayonnaise; it will be very tasty. Place in middle of platter, arrange rest of salad around it. You will enjoy the full flavor of each food.

You can also make this mustard mayonnaise for an added flavor by mixing together:

1 cup Hellman's mayonnaise
4 tsp Gulden's Diablo mustard
24 drops or less tabasco to taste
3 tsp Lea and Perrins Worcestershire sauce
3 tsp dry mustard

Rosa's Best Ever Tuna Fish Salad

utensils
mixing bowl
salad platter
serves 2-3

1 (7-oz) can good-quality white tuna fish, drained
2 tender inside stalks celery, minced fine
3 scallion bulbs, minced fine
salt and pepper to taste
2 tbsp Hellman's mayonnaise
Boston lettuce leaves
sprinkle of paprika

Mix tuna fish well, not keeping it in chunks. Combine with rest of ingredients, adding salt and pepper to taste. Serve in Boston lettuce leaves and decorate with sprinkle of paprika.

*"Stuffed Eggs" (see its recipe), go very well with this salad as do crisp radishes, green olives and kosher-style dill pickles.

Chopped Herring Salad

utensils
chopping bowl and chopper
wire strainer
makes about 1 cup

1 (8-oz) jar herring tidbits in wine sauce
1 hard-boiled egg
½ small onion, peeled
1 small tart apple, peeled
½ tsp white distilled vinegar to taste
2 hard-boiled eggs, peeled and separated

In the chopping bowl, chop egg and onion until fine. Add herring and apple and chop until mixture is chopped fine. Stir in about ½ tsp white vinegar.

Mince hard-boiled egg whites and push egg yolks through wire strainer. Make a round circle of the herring, decorate by alternating egg whites and egg yolks, spoke-fashion into a pinwheel.

Chopped herring makes a good first course and a good hors d'oeuvre especially when served with a good black bread.

165

Butter Sauce

Melt butter, pour over seasoned vegetable, discard white matter at bottom of pan.

Browned Butter Sauce

Clarify butter by melting it, being careful not to burn, pour off golden yellow butter, leave white dregs. One-half stick butter is enough for 2 cups vegetables.

Place clarified butter on medium heat, let foam, then brown. Remove as soon as it turns a nut color, don't let it get dark brown or burn, as it will be bitter. Pour over steamed hot vegetable.

Cream Sauce

Stir 2 tbsp melted butter into seasoned vegetable. Pour boiling cream over and bake in 350° oven about 10 min until cream is absorbed.

Cauliflower, brussels sprouts, broccoli, asparagus, and string beans all go well with any of the following sauces: butter sauce, browned butter sauce, cream sauce, "Foolproof White Sauce" (see its recipe), "Cheese Sauce" (see its recipe), "Best Ever Easy Hollandaise Sauce" (see its recipe) and "Lemon Butter Sauce" (see its recipe).

Brandy Sauce

utensils
  small bowl
  wooden spoon
makes ½ cup

½ cup Hellman's unsweetened mayonnaise
2 tsp tomato sauce
2 drops tabasco
4 tsp brandy

Gradually combine all the ingredients until smooth.

Don't add more brandy or tabasco, as it will impair the flavor.

This sauce is good on sliced tomatoes, "Asparagus Salad" (see its recipe) and with seafood.

166

an improved Hollandaise sauce

Béarnaise Sauce

utensils
    saucepan
    strainer
makes about 1 cup

2 large egg yolks
¼ lb butter
salt and pepper to taste

SEASONING LIQUID
½ cup white wine
1 tbsp tarragon vinegar or wine vinegar
    with ¼ tsp dried tarragon steeped in it
1 tsp minced onion
1 tsp minced parsley
pinch of dried tarragon

Cook seasoning liquid uncovered over moderate heat until there is only ¼ cup liquid left. Strain and cool. This can be done earlier. Use this liquid instead of lemon juice in the *"Best Ever Easy Hollandaise Sauce" (see its recipe).

for vegetables; a quickie

Sour Cream Sauce

cooking time 1-2 min

utensils
    saucepan
    strainer
makes 1 cup

1 hard-boiled egg yolk, strained
1 cup sour cream
2 tbsp butter
salt and pepper to taste

Push yolk with paper towel through strainer into sour cream, stir smooth. Gradually add butter on medium heat, being careful not to boil, as sour cream may curdle; heat, season with salt and pepper. When thoroughly hot, pour over the heated vegetables.

Good with string beans, cauliflower, or brussels sprouts.

167

Oilless Vinaigrette Sauce with Mayonnaise

utensils
 mixing bowl
 wooden spoon
 saucepan
 cups to steep herbs in
makes ½ cup

2 tbsp wine vinegar
1 tsp dry mustard
½ tsp each dried tarragon, dill and chervil
 each steeped in 1 tbsp boiling water 15
 min
pinch of salt
½ cup mayonnaise

Strain herbs into wine vinegar, mix into mayonnaise. Add salt.

For a real vinaigrette, add 6 tbsp oil.

This is delicious over sliced hard-boiled eggs seasoned with salt and pepper. It also makes tasty stuffing for hard-boiled eggs.

variations

Add sieved hard-boiled egg yolk to mayonnaise, 2 tbsp sour cream, then rest of ingredients. This is delicious over cold asparagus, fresh, frozen or canned, marinated in proportion of 2 tbsp wine vinegar to 6 tbsp oil. Chop hard-boiled egg white fine, decorate asparagus with it. Vary this by sprinkling fresh finely minced parsley.

Add 3 tbsp sour cream, pinch of sugar, grind of pepper to mayonnaise; change vinaigrette sauce by using 1 tsp lemon juice or wine instead of wine vinegar. This is good over cucumbers.

Substitute basil for tarragon in vinaigrette sauce, mix with mayonnaise. Marinate peeled, sliced tomatoes in oil and vinegar, (3 tbsp oil to 1 tbsp vinegar) about 15 min, add salt to taste before spooning on the seasoned mayonnaise.

Combine mayonnaise with 2 tbsp finely minced green onions, 2 tbsp finely minced fresh parsley, 2 tbsp sour cream, 1 tsp lemon juice, salt and pepper to taste.

Vary the above by substituting a good wet mustard to taste for the sour cream. This is good with cold fish.

Mix mayonnaise with sieved hard-boiled egg yolks, thinned with sweet cream or milk or lemon juice or sour cream or wine vinegar, depending on the dish it will garnish. You can add minced sweet or sour pickles, capers, or anchovies. You can also add finely minced hard-boiled egg whites. Test and taste.

The best way to sieve hard-boiled egg yolks is to use a paper towel to push yolks through strainer. This works like magic—so good, so quick.

fix ahead

Easy Homemade Mayonnaise

utensils
sieve
electric mixer or wooden
    spoon
small bowl
rubber spatula
makes about 1½ cups

3 hard-boiled egg yolks
1 tsp dry mustard
2 raw yolks
1 cup vegetable oil (olive or your favorite)
1 tsp lemon juice or wine vinegar or both
salt to taste

Sieve hard-boiled yolks by pushing with paper towel through strainer before mixing with mustard, gradually add raw yolks, beat on low in mixer or mix by hand until combined, which takes a second. Turn to high, beat for 1-2 min before gradually adding 1 tbsp oil, beat until absorbed, then add another tbsp oil, use rubber spatula to get mixture into beaters. Continue until all the oil has been added, being careful that each addition is absorbed before adding the next. You can pour more oil at a time as you continue.

When all oil has been added, add lemon juice and/or wine vinegar, ¼ tsp at a time, to taste; add salt to taste.

Lighten mayonnaise if you wish by gradually adding 2 tbsp boiling water to mayonnaise.

If the mayonnaise curdles, don't blow your top. Mix 1 tbsp very hot water into mayonnaise—this will smooth it out; if not, add another tbsp water and mix. This should do it.

169

can be frozen and reheated

Never-fail Hollandaise Sauce

cooking time about 10 min

utensils
saucepan
wooden spoon
cup with handle
makes about a cup

¾ cup butter
3 large egg yolks, broken up with fork
½-2 tsp lemon juice, to taste
1 tbsp cold water

There's more talk here than work, so don't be afraid to try.

To clarify butter, melt on low heat; off heat remove scum on top by floating small pieces of paper towels, then tilt saucepan carefully not to disturb particles on bottom, pour golden butter into cup with handle to make pouring easier later, leaving all particles on bottom which will not be used. You should have ½ cup clarified butter. Let cool to room temperature.

Combine eggs, lemon juice and water before placing on lowest possible heat, stir continuously until mixture thickens a little, which takes about 2 min. Move saucepan off and on heat if necessary to keep from getting too hot and scrambling the eggs.

Remove from heat; gradually, by drops, stirring gently all the while, start adding butter. Place back on lowest heat, slowly add butter, and as it is absorbed, continue adding butter, stirring, taking off and on heat if necessary, not adding more until previous addition is absorbed. Then start adding butter a little faster until all butter is used and sauce thickens.

Serve Hollandaise warm, not hot, and as soon as possible. You can keep it over lukewarm water ½-1 hr, or you can reheat it, adding a little at a time over low heat.

You can lighten Hollandaise by stirring in 1 tbsp hot water at the end.

170

Curdling is no problem with this sauce, although when butter is not clarified, it sometimes curdles. If sauce curdles, add 1 tbsp cold water and stir with wooden spoon until it becomes smooth again. If it doesn't smooth out, add another spoon. You can add as many as 3 tablespoons if necessary, but one usually does the trick.

Best Ever
Easy Hollandaise Sauce

cooking time about 10 min

utensils
strainer
saucepan
wooden spoon
makes about a cup

2 large egg yolks
½-2 tsp lemon juice, strained, or seasoning liquid in *"Béarnaise Sauce" (see its recipe)
¼ lb butter
salt and pepper to taste

Divide butter into 3 parts, let soften somewhat at room temperature. Add strained juice to yolks, salt and pepper. Before placing on lowest heat, stir with wooden spoon, taking off and on heat. Eggs will thicken somewhat, but do not let mixture get hot as you will have scrambled eggs instead of a sauce.

Add 1 piece butter, continue to stir, cook off and on heat; when butter has melted and sauce starts to thicken, add the second piece, continue as before until all butter has been added and sauce is a lovely thick consistency. This does not take long. Correct seasoning, add more lemon juice as you like, or if sauce is too thick, add 1-2 tbsp hot water.

Hollandaise sauce is served warm, not hot. Keep it over warm water, not hot, if it has to wait.

Hollandaise can be frozen and reheated on very low heat or over hot water by defrosting and heating 2 tbsp, gradually beating in the rest a spoonful at a time.

171

good on vegetables

Lemon Butter Sauce

cooking time about 10 min

utensils
saucepan

makes about ½ cup

⅛ cup lemon juice, pinch of salt, pinch of pepper
½ stick butter (4 tbsp) divided into 8 pieces
1-2 tbsp chicken broth, canned or fresh

Boil lemon juice seasoned with salt and pepper to reduce to 1 tbsp. Off heat, beat in 2 pieces butter, one at a time, place on simmer, beat in pieces of butter, one at a time until all has been used. Remove immediately from heat. Before serving, beat in heated broth, a tiny bit at a time.

Cheese Sauce

cooking time about 20 min

utensils
saucepan

makes about 1 cup

1 tbsp butter, melted
1 tbsp flour
1 cup milk
¼ cup swiss or cheddar cheese, grated, or half and half, the other being parmesan
salt and pepper to taste

Make "White Sauce" (see its recipe) as usual, remove from heat, beat in grated cheese until it has melted in sauce. Add salt, pepper to taste. For some vegetables you can vary this by adding a pinch of nutmeg.

good over cauliflower or string beans

Easy Cheese Sauce

cooking time about 10 min

utensils
saucepan

makes 1 cup

4 oz. Velveeta cheese, cut into pieces
1 cup milk

Stir, heat Velveeta added to milk until cheese has melted and sauce is hot.

Can be varied by adding tsp white wine or vermouth before cooking.

172

for smart people

Foolproof White Sauce

cooking time 10 min

utensils
saucepan

makes 1 cup

GUIDE TO THICKNESS
thin sauce
1 tbsp flour to 1 tbsp butter to 1 cup milk
medium sauce
1½ tbsp flour to 1½ tbsp butter to 1 cup milk
thick sauce
2 tbsp flour to 2 tbsp butter to 1 cup milk
very thick sauce
2½ tbsp flour to 2½ tbsp butter to 1 cup milk

Use whatever amount flour, butter and milk you need for the kind of sauce you need.

Melt the butter; off heat, stir in flour, milk. Return to heat, stir, cook on medium, bring to boil, reduce heat to low, stir, cook 10 min to take away the raw flour taste and to get a smooth, creamy sauce.

Handy Cream Sauce

cooking time 10 min

utensils
saucepan

makes 2 cups

3 tbsp butter
3 tbsp flour
1½ cups milk
½ cup heavy whipping cream
salt and pepper to taste

Melt butter, off heat stir in flour, then milk. Place on medium heat, stir, cook 8 min, stir in cream, cook 2 min before seasoning with salt and pepper. Pour over vegetables.

Vary by adding strained lemon juice to taste, or by adding chopped hard-boiled egg whites to the sauce, then push egg yolks with paper towel through strainer to decorate it.

If sauce has to wait, mix it now and then or cover with a little melted butter to keep skin from forming, then reheat.

This goes well with broccoli, cauliflower, asparagus or brussels sprouts.

173

especially good with crab fingers or other cold seafood

Brandied Mustard Sauce

utensils
  mixing bowl
  wooden spoon
makes 1¼ cups

1 cup unsweetened mayonnaise
1 tsp dry mustard
½ tsp yellow wet mustard
1 tsp wine vinegar
4 tbsp lime or lemon juice
1 tsp brandy
½ tsp sugar
salt to taste
⅛ tsp pepper

Gradually mix mayonnaise into dry mustard so it does not lump. Combine rest of the ingredients, mix thoroughly. Correct seasoning.

If you are lucky enough to get crab fingers, dip them one by one into sauce and eat. This is a real delicacy.

English Mustard

this mustard is hot; fix ahead

utensils
  bowl
  wooden spoon
makes about 1 tbsp

2 tsp dry mustard
1½ tsp cold water

Mix mustard and cold water together until smooth.

This basic proportion can be increased to any quantity.

Mustard Sauce for Shrimp

utensils
  mixing bowl
  wooden spoon
makes 1 cup

1 cup Hellman's unsweetened mayonnaise
2 tsp wet mustard
1 egg yolk
½ tsp wine vinegar

Either mix in a blender or by hand.

Winey Mustard Sauce

utensils
  mixing bowl
  wooden spoon
makes 1⅔ cups

1 cup unsweetened mayonnaise
½ tsp dry mustard
1 tsp wet mustard
½ cup sour cream
½ tsp Durkee's dressing
1 tsp lemon juice
1 tbsp wine

Mix mayonnaise into dry mustard, stir in the remaining
ingredients. Add sour cream last.

fix ahead

Snappy Sauce

utensils
  mixing bowl
  wooden spoon
makes ½ cup

½ cup unsweetened mayonnaise
2 tsp prepared mustard
1½ tsp prepared horseradish
salt and pepper to taste

Mix mayonnaise with rest of ingredients.

This sauce is fine with seafood, such as shrimp, crabmeat, or fried or broiled fish.

Fisherman's Sauce

utensils
mixing bowl
wooden spoon
makes ½ cup

¼ cup unsweetened mayonnaise
2 tbsp chili sauce
¼ cup sour cream
2 tsp lemon juice
dash of tabasco
⅛ tsp marjoram

Gradually stir ingredients into mayonnaise.

Serve with fish or seafood.

good with shrimp; fix ahead

Le Maise Sauce

utensils
mixing bowl
wooden spoon
2 forks

½ tsp grated onion
1 tbsp chopped pimento
1 tbsp chopped celery
1 cup unsweetened mayonnaise
½ cup chili sauce
¼ cup India or pickle relish
1½ tsp prepared mustard
1 tsp Worcestershire sauce
½ tsp paprika
salt and pepper to taste

Mix all ingredients into mayonnaise. Stir into 2 lb *"Steamed Shrimp" (see its recipe), using forks so as not to crush the shrimp.

Serve in Boston lettuce cups, and decorate with slices of 2 hard-boiled eggs.

176

Cocktail Sauce

utensils
   mixing bowl
   wooden spoon
makes 1 cup sauce

¼ cup chili sauce
½ cup ketchup
¼ cup lemon juice
½ tsp white prepared horseradish

Blend all ingredients together. Serve with shrimp, crab-meat or other seafood. This is a fresh-tasting sauce.

The sauce can be served in individual small dishes along with the seafood or in Boston or romaine leaves which serve as a cup for the sauce and look pretty, too.

fix ahead

Creole Sauce for Shrimp

cooking time 1½ hr
utensils
   saucepan without lid
makes about 3 cups

1½ tbsp minced onion
4 cloves garlic
2 tbsp vegetable oil
½ cup diced ham
2 cups tomato puree
1 1-lb can or 2 cups fresh tomatoes
2 tsp Worcestershire sauce
2 bay leaves
½ tsp dried thyme
¼ tsp salt and pepper to taste
¼ tsp sugar
½ tsp bitters
½ tsp filet powder (optional)

Sauté onion gently in oil, add the remaining ingredients except filet powder. Simmer uncovered 1½ hrs.

Add filet powder to thicken, but do not boil.

Serve over *"Steamed Shrimp" (see its recipe).

177

Seasoned Butters

These seasoned butters are very easy to prepare, but it is best to make them early in the morning, or the day before. This gives the butter a chance to season and to harden, which makes it easy to handle.

SEASONED BUTTER 1

1 tbsp butter, softened at room
    temperature
⅛ tsp garlic powder
¼ tsp flour

SEASONED BUTTER 2

1 tbsp butter
¼ tsp flour
¼ tsp dried tarragon

SEASONED BUTTER 3

1 tbsp butter
¼ tsp flour
⅛ tsp ginger
¼ tsp herb seasoning

SEASONED BUTTER 4

1 tbsp butter
¼ tsp flour
⅛ tsp ginger
½ tsp sherry wine
¼ tsp basil

SEASONED BUTTER 5

2 tbsp butter
¼ tsp flour
½ tsp Worcestershire sauce
¼ tsp dry mustard
⅛ tsp garlic powder
¼ tsp lemon juice
1 drop tabasco sauce

SEASONED BUTTER 6

2 tbsp butter
¼ tsp flour
¼ tsp wet mustard
½ tsp Worcestershire sauce
⅛ tsp garlic powder
½ tsp sherry wine

SEASONED BUTTER 7

2 tbsp butter
¼ tsp flour
½ tsp Worcestershire Sauce
½ tsp wet mustard
⅛ tsp garlic powder

Prepare all these versions the same way. Mix together with teaspoon; then push seasoned butter off teaspoon onto wax paper and put in refrigerator to harden. When ready to use, slice off thin slices to place on top of broiled fish, seafood, hamburgers or chicken.

One tbsp seasoned butter will cover about 16 baby lobster tails or langostinas (see "Sweet Broiled Langostinas or Baby Lobster Tails").

178

fix ahead

Black Cherry Sauce

cooking time about 10 min

utensils
saucepan
small bowl
makes about 1 cup

1 cup red burgundy wine
¼ cup sugar
1 tsp water
2 tsp cornstarch
1 cup canned, pitted black cherries, strained

Stir, cook wine and sugar until it boils, reduce heat, cook 2 min. Off heat, combine water and cornstarch, add a little hot wine mixture; then, off heat, stir into wine sauce in saucepan.

Place back on heat, stir, bring back to boil, reduce to low, cook 3 min, until sauce is clear and has a little body.

This can be made early. When ready to serve, heat sauce, add cherries, heat, serve in pretty sauce dish with a spoon. It is delicious spooned over "Spiced Roast Duck" (see its recipe), or just as enjoyable over nicely roasted 1½-lb chickens, see recipe "Juicy Roasted Chicken."

for chickens or Cornish Hens

Southern Barbecue Sauce

utensils
screw-top jar
makes about ¾ cup

½ tsp ginger
1 tbsp all-purpose flour
¼ cup chili sauce
2 tbsp sweet pickle juice
4 tbsp lemon juice
2 tsp Worcestershire sauce
2 tbsp honey
3 drops tabasco
1 tbsp paprika
½ tsp onion powder
large pinch salt

Put lemon juice in screw-top jar, add flour and dried ginger, shake until combined. Add rest of ingredients and shake.

179

Basting Sauce for Broiled Chicken or Fish

cooking *time* long enough to
melt butter

utensils
small saucepan
makes enough for 2 broilers or
4 filets fish

2 tbsp melted butter
¼ tsp ginger
¼ tsp dry mustard
¼ tsp paprika
½ tsp flour
¼ tsp salt

Mix all ingredients together, use as a basting sauce.

fix ahead

Barbecue Sauce

utensils
jar with lid
makes ½ cup

½ tsp dried ginger mixed into ½ cup
ketchup or chili sauce
2 tbsp vegetable oil
2 tbsp lemon juice or bourbon
1 tbsp honey
¼ tsp ground all spice

Mix ginger gradually into ketchup so it doesn't lump;
add rest of ingredients and shake in jar to combine.

Store in refrigerator until needed.

fix ahead

Hot Barbecue Sauce

utensils
jar with lid
makes 1 cup

¼ tsp dried mustard mixed into ½ cup
ketchup
¼ cup sweet pickle juice
¼ cup vegetable oil
¼ cup Worcestershire sauce
¼ cup prepared mustard
¼ cup honey
juice from 1 lemon, strained
few drops tabasco (optional)

Mix dried mustard gradually into ketchup so it doesn't
lump; add rest of ingredients and shake in jar to
combine.

Store in refrigerator until needed.

180

fix ahead

No-cook
Horseradish Sauce

cooking time no cooking needed, but can be heated

½ cup sour cream
1 tsp or more prepared horseradish drained

utensils
   bowl
   saucepan if you heat
     sauce
makes ½ cup

Stir together, taste to correct amount of horseradish.

Can be heated gently over low heat; don't boil or it will curdle, but serve hot.

Good served with short ribs or brisket.

Cooked Horseradish Sauce

cooking time 5-7 min

utensils
   saucepan
makes ½ cup

1 tbsp melted butter
1 tbsp flour
½ cup milk
1 tsp horseradish to taste

Melt butter, do not brown. Off heat stir in flour, add milk, place back on heat, cook, stir about 5 min. Remove from heat, stir in horseradish, serve hot. Good with boiled beef.

181

fix ahead

Quickie Tomato Sauce with White Wine

cooking time 30 min

utensils
  saucepan
makes 2⅓ cups

2 (6-oz) cans vegetable juice
1 (10½-oz) can marinara sauce
3 tbsp sweet vermouth or sweet sauterne
¼ tsp salt
1 tsp sugar to taste
pepper to taste

Bring all ingredients to boil, while stirring, turn to simmer, simmer without lid 20-30 min.

Quickie Tomato Sauce with Sherry

cooking time 30 min

utensils
  saucepan
makes 3 cups

2 (8-oz) cans Arturo sauce
2 (8-oz) cans vegetable juice
1 tbsp sherry
2-3 drops tabasco
salt and pepper to taste

Bring ingredients to boil, reduce to simmer. Simmer 25 min. Correct seasoning.

Tangy Tomato Sauce

cooking time 20-30 min

utensils
wire strainer
saucepan without lid
wooden spoon
makes about 2 cups

2 (14½-oz) cans pear-shaped tomatoes or fresh tomatoes in season only
1 (8-oz) can vegetable juice
1 large bay leaf
1 allspice
½ tsp dried basil
1¼ tsp salt to taste
pepper to taste
2½ tsp sugar
1 clove garlic, peeled
1 medium whole onion, peeled

Strain tomatoes through wire strainer pushing through pulp and leaving seeds. Add all ingredients, place on high heat, bring to boil, reduce heat to low, simmer about 20-30 min until sauce is thick.

This is a good fresh-tasting sauce.

Thickenings

Cornstarch, Potato Starch, Arrowroot, Flour

½ tbsp cornstarch, arrowroot, or potato starch to 1 cup liquid makes a thin sauce or gravy.

1 tbsp cornstarch, arrowroot, or potato starch to 1 cup liquid makes a thick sauce or gravy.

1 tbsp flour to 1 cup liquid makes a thin gravy or sauce.

1½ tbsp flour to 1 cup liquid makes a medium gravy or sauce.

2 tbsp flour to 1 cup liquid makes a thick gravy or sauce.

2½ tbsp flour to 1 cup liquid makes a thick white sauce.

How to Thicken with Flour

To thicken with flour, take a small amount of cold liquid you want to thicken, put into screw-top jar, add proper amount of flour, shake, then pour into liquid. Stir, cook over medium heat until it boils, reduce to simmer; simmer 10 min, stirring now and then. This helps to get rid of the raw flour taste as well as provide the right consistency. Remember, to keep from getting lumps, always add the flour to the liquid.

You can add the new granulated flour to cold liquid and cook without getting lumps.

How to Thicken with Cornstarch, Arrowroot or Potato Starch

Mix a little cold water with the thickening and stir into food you are heating and wish to thicken. Cook, stir, bring to a boil, reduce heat to low and cook about 5 min until liquid clears. Cook only until it clears as all the starches thin out with long cooking or stirring.

Butter Balls

Two tbsp flour to 2 tbsp softened (not melted) butter or margarine to 1 cup liquid make a thickening of nice consistency, nice body and not too thick. Mix together butter and flour thoroughly, push off tiny balls from spoon on top of liquid you wish to thicken, cook, stir on low heat, adding tiny balls until you have right consistency.

184

Egg Yolks

Three egg yolks will thicken 1 cup liquid. Off heat gradually stir a little of the hot liquid into the egg yolks, then gradually stir back into rest of liquid. Cook but do not boil to get right consistency. Boiling curdles the eggs. It takes only a few min to thicken with egg yolks.

Beef Drippings

Use 2 tbsp beef drippings (fat) to 2 tbsp flour to 1 cup liquid. Gradually stir flour into drippings. Off heat add liquid; replace on heat, cook, stir until gravy is right consistency.

fix ahead

Favorite Imperial Crab

cooking time 15-20 min
    preheat oven 375°

utensils
    baking shells
    mixing bowl
serves 4-6

1 can lump crabmeat, shells removed
1 tsp wet mustard
1 tsp dry mustard
½ cup unsweetened mayonnaise
¼ cup heavy whipping cream
1 tsp Worcestershire sauce to taste
1 tsp sherry
salt and pepper to taste
2 drops tabasco
1 tbsp finely minced parsley
butter to dot crab
paprika to sprinkle on crab

        Combine all ingredients before adding very carefully to crab meat, correct seasoning, spoon into shells, dot with butter, sprinkle paprika on. Bake 15-20 min in preheated oven.

fix ahead

Deviled Crab

cooking time 12-15 min
    preheat oven 400°

utensils
    mixing bowl
    4 baking shells or dishes
serves 4-6

1 lb lump crab meat, shells removed
8 tbsp (½ cup) unsweetened mayonnaise
1 tbsp Durkee's dressing
1 tbsp Lea and Perrins Worcestershire sauce
⅛ tsp tabasco to taste
1 tsp dry mustard
⅛ tsp pepper
1 tbsp finely minced white scallion bulb or onion
2 tbsp green pepper, finely minced
1 tbsp prepared mustard
1 red pimento, canned, minced
buttered crumbs to dot top

        Carefully mix all ingredients together before adding to the crab meat, being very careful not to mash crab meat. Dot with buttered crumbs. Bake about 12-15 min.

186

Crabmeat Imperial

cooking time 15-20 min
preheat oven 350°

utensils
large mixing bowl
baking sheet
6 shells or baking dishes
serves 4-6

1 (1-lb) can of lump crab meat
1 tbsp butter
1 tbsp flour
1 cup light cream
2 tbsp sherry
1 egg yolk
½ tsp Accent
¼ tsp salt to taste
2 drops tabasco or pinch of red or black pepper
2 pieces canned pimento, minced
about 2 tbsp unsweetened mayonnaise
sprinkle of paprika

Pick over crab meat and remove any shells, being careful not to crush crab meat. Gently add pimento.

Melt butter, off heat stir in flour, then cream and sherry, return to low heat, stir, cook about 5 min. Off heat stir in the egg yolk, place back on low heat (do not boil), stir 2-3 min before adding tabasco, Accent and salt.

Divide crab meat into shells, spoon sauce over them; with knife, smear mayonnaise on top, sprinkle a little paprika on.

Bake in preheated oven on baking sheet for 15-20 min, when they will be hot and bubbly.

You can vary this dish by adding diced shrimp langostinas or baby lobster tails, steamed first (see "Steamed Shrimp" and "Steamed Langostinas or Baby Lobster Tails"). This would then be Seafood Imperial.

Maryland Crab Cakes

cooking time 15-20 min

utensils
skillet
mixing bowl
serves 4-6

1 lb lumb crab meat, picked over and shells removed
¼ cup unsweetened mayonnaise
1 large egg stirred with fork
¼ tsp freshly ground pepper
½ tsp salt to taste
¾ tsp dry mustard
4 tbsp butter, margarine or vegetable shortening to fry

Mix all ingredients lightly, adding very carefully to crab meat. Shape cakes with your hands or better still drop with spoon into heated skillet with some of fat in it. Do not crowd crab cakes, brown nicely on both sides, serve hot.

"Cole Slaw" (see its recipe) goes very nicely with crab cakes.

Maryland Crab Soup

cooking time 15-30 min

utensils
  skillet
  saucepan
serves 4-5

1 (1-lb) can lump crab meat
4 cups clam broth
2 cups water
½ cup minced onion or scallions
4 tsp paprika
½ cup long grain, converted rice
4 tbsp oil (peanut or your favorite)
1 tsp dried oregano
½ tsp tabasco
salt and pepper to taste
1 small firm potato, Irish cobbler, peeled
    and minced fine, set aside in water to
    keep from discoloring
¼ cup butter or margarine

Bring clam broth and water to boil; in the meatime, fry onion in oil until soft but not browned. Add paprika and continue stirring. Add rice, stir, cook 3 min, add to broth, then add finely minced potatoes and rest of ingredients, except crab meat, bring to boil, reduce to medium, cook until rice and potatoes are done but still firm. Add crab meat, correct seasoning.

This dish tastes even better the second day when everything is blended into a delicious taste.

Saucy Lobster

cooking time about 40 min

utensils
kettle
colander
scissors
paring knife
skillet
saucepan
small bowl
serves about 4

*"Steamed Rice" (see its recipe)
*1½ lb steamed langostinas (see recipe "Steamed Langostinas or Baby Lobster Tails")
*1 lb steamed baby lobster tails (see recipe "Steamed Langostinas or Baby Lobster Tails")
2 tbsp peanut or other oil
2 cloves finely crushed garlic
2 cups canned, boiled chicken broth
¼ lb lean ground pork
½ tsp sugar
pinch of ginger
⅛ tsp salt
2 minced scallions, green stalks and bulbs
1 tbsp and 1 tsp soy sauce
2 tbsp sherry
3 tbsp cornstarch mixed with 2 tbsp cold water
2 eggs beaten slightly with fork

Heat ground pork in oil with garlic (don't burn), separate pork, cook; this takes about 5 min. Combine sugar, ginger, salt, broth defatted by floating small pieces of paper towels on top, sherry, soy sauce and cornstarch mixture. Bring to boil, reduce heat, stir (don't overcook), until sauce is clear and thick, add scallions and lobster, heat, pour eggs into sauce, heat a second, remove from heat and stir. Some of the eggs will be absorbed into the sauce and some will be stringlike.

Serve with rice.

This lobster freezes well; it also takes quite well to reheating. The frozen lobsters are particularly sweet; when you can't get Maine lobsters, these are always available at good supermarkets in the frozen fish department. Be sure they are frozen, uncooked and have their shells on when you buy them.

190

Steamed Langostinas or Baby Lobster Tails

1. Buy 2 lb frozen langostinas or lobster tails; don't defrost and don't peel. (Note: langostinas are lobster tails from baby langostas, a spiny South or Central American lobster, and are smaller than ordinary baby lobster tails.

2. Bring to rapid boil, 8 cups water, ¼ cup white vinegar and 1 tbsp salt, drop in seafood, bring back to rapid boil, boil 2 min. Taste to be sure seafood is cooked.

3. Immediately remove to colander, run cold water over them to stop cooking.

4. After cooling, which takes only a few min, cut lengthwise down middle of top shell with scissors to make it easier to remove the langostinas or baby lobsters inside with your fingers. Remove dark veins with paring knife. Remove shells from baby lobster tails.

5. Remember not to overcook them, not to steam too many at a time; don't cook too long. Cool instantly the fastest way by plunging them into large bowl of ice and running cold water over them.

fix ahead

Seafood Delight

cooking time 20-30 min+
preparation time

utensils
large saucepot
large bowl
serves 6-8

SEAFOOD INGREDIENTS
2 lb fresh or defrosted frozen shrimp
2 lb frozen baby lobster tails in shell, defrosted under running cold water
2 lb frozen langostinas in shell, defrosted under running cold water
8 cups water
1 tbsp salt
¼ cup distilled vinegar

This is most important: be sure to save the water the seafood is cooked in! Do not throw it out!

Bring seasoned water to boil, gradually drop in shrimp, bring back to boil; boil 2 min only. Save shrimp broth by pouring shrimp into colander over large bowl, set bowl with shrimp broth aside while you run cold water over shrimp to stop any further cooking. Place in refrigerator until ready to use.

Cook baby lobster tails in boiling shrimp water after adding additional water to make 8 cups. Don't put in lobsters until broth boils rapidly, and only boil them 2 min. Repeat as with the shrimp; be sure to save the broth.

Repeat with langostinas just what you did with shrimp and baby lobster tails; be sure to save broth for the soup, while you cool langostinas quickly and refrigerate.

Remove seafood from refrigerator; shell, devein and cut shrimp into thirds, refrigerate again while you make the soup.

SOUP INGREDIENTS

½ cup minced scallions or onions
4 tbsp oil
4 tsp paprika
4 large bay leaves
4 whole allspice
2 tsp oregano
½ tsp tabasco

¼ tsp salt
pepper to taste
½ cup converted rice
1 cup firm potatoes, minced fine
8 cups leftover seafood broth
lump of butter size of a walnut

Fry onion in oil to soften but not brown, add paprika, stir in rice, cook 1 min before stirring in the seafood

192

broth and bring to boil. Add the rest of the ingredients except pepper, bring to boil, reduce heat to medium, cook until potatoes and rice are firm but cooked; don't let them get mushy.

Add seafood, bring to boil, correct seasoning, sprinkle pepper on, remove from heat. This stew can be served at once, or it can be cooled and ripened in refrigerator overnight to blend the flavors, reheated and eaten with crusty French or Italian bread.

You can vary this by adding 1 cup rich cream and heating, correcting with a little more herbs and seasoning as the cream makes the stew a little bland.

Lobster Marengo

cooking time 25-30 min

utensils
saucepan
wooden spoon

serves 4

*"Rice—The French Method" (see its recipe)
1 can Campbell's frozen shrimp soup, defrosted
½ cup rich whipping cream
1 canned whole pimento, minced
1½ tbsp brandy
1½ tsp sherry
8 drops tabasco
1 (10-oz) can lobster or 1 lb *"Steamed Shrimp" (see its recipe)
½ can lump crab meat, shells picked out (optional)

Stir cream into shrimp soup, add rest of ingredients except seafood. Gently add seafood, correct seasoning, heat, but don't boil, until thoroughly heated. Serve over rice.

Instead of serving over rice, you can serve this dish over toast or put into shells and heat in 375° oven about 15 min.

193

Sweet Broiled Langostinas or Baby Lobster Tails

cooking time 3-4 min
preheat broiler

utensils
individual fireproof baking dishes

serves 4

1-2 lb frozen lobster tails or langostinas, defrosted in refrigerator
*one of the "Seasoned Butters" (see their recipe)

Make seasoned butter early, the day before if you wish; refrigerate.

Remove langostinas from shells by cutting bright side of shells lengthwise and lifting out langostinas with your fingers; cut off flippers first, put langostinas back into shells, place in individual baking dishes, season with a little salt.

If using baby lobster tails, remove from shell by cutting shell lengthwise and lifting out. Place in individual baking dishes, sprinkle a little salt to season and put in refrigerator until ready to broil.

Cut small thin slices of the firm prepared seasoned butter and arrange on langostinas or baby lobster tails. Place on second shelf of oven and broil 3-4 min, no longer. Serve with sprinkle of pepper.

The pretty langostina shells will add a colorful note to your dining table.

194

the best ever; fix ahead

Steamed Shrimp

cooking time 3 min

utensils
    large saucepan
    colander
serves 4-6

2 lb shrimp
8 cups water
1 tbsp salt
¼ cup white vinegar

If using frozen shrimp, defrost them under cold tap water before cooking.

Bring water, vinegar and salt to rolling, rapid boil. Gradually drop shrimp in. Bring back to boil, start timing immediately, boil 2 min, taste a shrimp. If not cooked, boil 1 min longer. The shrimp should be cooked in 3 min—never more than 4. Remove from heat immediately, place in colander, run cold water over them to stop cooking.

Remove shells, devein (remove dark vein with sharp paring knife), refrigerate until needed. These shrimp are never mealy.

An excellent fish seller, who works at a tiny place next to where the commercial fishermen dock, told me Florida lobster are just as sweet as Maine ones, and to prove it, he steamed some just 12 min, plunged them immediately into gobs of crushed ice to stop the cooking. I tasted them, sweet as sugar, juicy as a dream! He does shrimp the same way, steaming 3 min, no more!

Batter-fried Shrimp

cooking time about ½ hr

utensils
    heavy skillet
    homemade rack for drain-
      ing shrimp
    baking sheet
    large mixing bowl
    small bowl
makes 6-9

3-4 lb large shrimp
peanut, or other oil, enough to fill skillet to
    ¼ inch of top
2 large or 3 medium egg yolks
1 cup tap water
1 cup flour

Remove shells, leaving tail shells attached. Slit shrimp to tails but leave tail shells attached, store in refrigerator.

Make draining rack by putting one rack on top of the other in opposite directions so that shrimp won't fall through, place on baking sheet.

Make well in flour, put egg yolks in, start mixing flour in, add water, gradually stir in all flour. The batter will be a little lumpy; don't beat smooth as this will toughen the batter. Set aside.

Put some flour in a bowl, set aside.

Heat oil in skillet, test if hot enough by dropping in small piece of bread; if it rises to top immediately, it is ready.

Lift shrimp by tails, dip in flour, shake, dip them into batter, drop into oil. Continue to drop, one at a time until 4-5 have been added. As each shrimp cooks, which takes about 3-5 min, remove with tongs, place on rack to drain a few seconds, then serve 1 person at a time, so shrimp do not get cold.

Dipping Sauce for Shrimp

1½ cans canned or fresh clam broth
4 tbsp sherry
¼ cup soy sauce
½ cup water
½ tsp fresh grated ginger
½ tbsp fine grated white horseradish
½ tsp grated white radish

Heat all ingredients except horseradish and grated radish together; put horseradish and grated radish in bottoms of individual bowls large enough for dipping. Pour heated ingredients into bowls.

Hold fried shrimp by their tails, dip into sauce. Happy eating.

As an alternate dipping sauce, serve "Cocktail Sauce" (see its recipe) hot or cold.

fix ahead

Shrimp and Crabmeat Casseroles

cooking time about 10 min
preheat oven 400°

utensils
mixing bowl
individual small baking dishes
serves 3-4

½ lb lump crab meat
*8 medium-sized "Steamed Shrimp" (see its recipe)
⅓ cup unsweetened mayonnaise
½ cup rich whipping cream
salt and pepper to taste
butter to dot crab meat
sprinkle of paprika

Shell and devein shrimp; cut into 1/3-inch pieces.

Combine mayonnaise and whipping cream into smooth sauce. With two forks, mix the sauce into crab meat and shrimp. Correct seasoning.

Mound crab meat mixture in individual small baking dishes, dot with butter, sprinkle some paprika on. Bake about 10-15 min until top is golden brown and heated through.

Crepes with Shrimp

cooking time 3 min to steam shrimp, to fry pancakes 15 min
preheat oven 400°

utensils
6½" skillet (teflon is fine)
mixing bowl
2 spatulas
dish towel
natural bristle brush
saucepan
shallow baking dish
¼ cup measuring cup
slotted spoon or strainer
makes about 24 small crepes

4 large eggs
1 cup skim milk
1 cup flour
1 tsp salt
vegetable shortening to grease skillet
*1 lb peeled, diced "Steamed Shrimp" (see its recipe)
2 cans Campbell's frozen cream of shrimp soup
¼ cup whipping cream
6 water chestnuts, sliced thin
2 tbsp finely chopped celery
4 tbsp finely chopped scallions
2 tbsp sherry
¼ tsp tabasco
¼ tsp salt to taste
grated parmesan cheese

To make crepes, make well in salted flour, put the eggs in, gradually stir flour in, then milk.

Preheat teflon skillet, otherwise brush fat on, pour a little less than ¼ cup batter, rotating it to cover bottom of skillet, bake on both sides, not browning.

To make filling and sauce, add sherry to defrosted shrimp soup, stir in cream, diced shrimp and rest of ingredients except parmesan cheese. Heat, but do not boil; with slotted spoon or strainer, remove moist shrimp and rest of solids to fill crepes, leaving the sauce to use later.

Fill crepes, roll up and close, turning sides down, place in baking dish with folded sides down, dribble some sauce over them (don't cover them with sauce), save some sauce to use later, sprinkle grated cheese over them lightly. Bake in oven about 10 min. Heat the extra sauce to serve along with the hot crepes.

198

Shrimp Marinara

cooking time 15 min

utensils
   saucepan
serves 4-6

*2 lb "Steamed Shrimp" (see its recipe), peeled and deveined
1 no. 2 can tomatoes
1 (7¾-oz) can tomato sauce
1 tsp sugar
2 large cloves garlic
½ tsp dried oregano
1 tbsp fresh parsley, minced
½ cup white wine (sauterne is good)
¾ tsp salt to taste
pepper to taste

Combine all ingredients except shrimp and parsley, bring to boil, reduce to simmer 15 min to blend the flavors.

Add steamed shrimp, bring to boil, serve, sprinkling minced parsley over them.

You can vary this by using a 1-lb can of Del Monte stewed tomatoes in place of the can of tomatoes.

a seafood and chicken delight; fix ahead

Paella

cooking time about 1½ hr
   preheat oven 350°

utensils
   skillet
   steamer
   round shallow metal bak-
      ing dish
serves 4-5

1 (2½-lb) chicken, cut into serving pieces,
   salted with 1 tsp salt, room temperature
*1 lb "Steamed Shrimps" (see its recipe)
4 tbsp or more oil or vegetable shortening
12 fresh littleneck clams, steamed, or 1
   (15-oz) can Tilghman's New England-
   style steamed clams in the shell
¼ cup minced green pepper
¼ cup minced onion
¼ cup minced celery
1 canned pimento, minced
1 fresh or canned tomato, peeled and
   chopped, seeds removed
2 tbsp butter
1 cup rice
3 cups broth (half canned chicken broth,
   half clam broth from can of clams or
   steamed clams)
¼-½ tsp saffron
1 large clove garlic, peeled, halved
1 tsp salt
1 cup fresh or frozen green peas
4 slices any Smithfield type ham, or some
   hot Spanish sausage

Cut chicken at room temperature into serving pieces;
   season with 1 tsp salt. Strain clams out of broth in
   can, cut black snouts off.

Brown chicken in oil, add garlic to flavor it (don't burn,
   as garlic tastes unpleasant if burned). Reduce heat
   to low, place foil over skillet, put lid on, fry until
   chicken is tender, about ½-¾ hr. Set chicken aside
   on plate, remove fat from skillet, swish clam broth
   and chicken broth to get all the good brownings in.
   Set aside in bowl while you wipe out skillet.

Fry pepper, onion, celery separately about 3 min each,
   don't brown (celery, pepper should be crisp while
   onion should be soft), last, fry chopped tomato 2
   min and set that aside too. The pimento does not
   need to be fried.

200

*Steam peas (see "Steaming," "Tested Times for Steamings Vegetables" and "Tested Times for Steaming Frozen Vegetables").

Wash out skillet, put in butter, stir in rice, cook about 5 min, don't brown, stir in saffron. Add enough broth to cover rice, bring to boil, reduce heat to low. Cook until broth evaporates, add more broth, repeat until rice is firm, tender but not mushy. Run fork through rice to keep it from sticking.

Place rice in baking dish (paella dish).

With 2 forks, stir in onion, celery, tomato, green pepper and pimento, precooked Smithfield ham in bite-size pieces, add peas to rice; if you use sausage instead of ham, arrange it around the rice. Mix shrimp into paella by sticking them into the rice, arrange chicken in and out of the rice, last arrange clams in shells on the rice. This should look like a picture "good enough to eat." Pour rest of broth in.

You can heat at once in the oven until paella is thoroughly hot and there is no broth left. Or you can place in refrigerator until you wish to heat and eat.

This is a lovely party dish with all the work done early.

Littleneck Clams in Wine Sauce

cooking time about 5 min

utensils
saucepan
slotted spoon
serves 4

4 doz fresh or canned littleneck clams, for big eaters, 2 doz for an appetizer
1 can chicken broth or clam broth with sand removed
4 tbsp butter
½ cup dry white wine (vermouth is good)

Wash clams.

Bring to a boil broth, white wine and butter, add clams, bring back to boil, boil gently until shells pop open. With slotted spoon, remove clams to deep soup bowls, strain broth over them.

If you use canned clams, combine as usual, but just heat after removing the snouts, as they have been cooked already.

Serve with crusty bread.

Baked Fish

cooking time 20-30 min

utensils
  baking pan
  saucepan
serves 2

1 whole, medium-size rock fish, striped bass, trout or red snapper
sprinkle of salt
grind of pepper
1 medium onion, sliced thin
½ carrot, sliced thin and parboiled
butter to dot fish
2 tbsp white wine, milk or water
butter to smear baking pan
2 pieces lemon

Sprinkle salt on fish, put in refrigerator to marinate ½ hr.

Arrange the fish in baking pan with onion on fish and carrot around it. Dot with butter, bake about 20-30 min, basting with butter and heated wine, water or milk. Test with fork to see that fish is cooked but not dry. Grind some pepper on, spoon some of the sauce on, add lemon, decorate with carrot, serve.

Sautéed Fish

cooking time about 10 min

utensils
  skillet
serves 2

2 small croakers, porgies, bass, flounder, butter fish, Norfolk spots, or red snapper
1 tsp salt
pepper
2-4 tbsp vegetable shortening and butter, half and half
milk to dip fish in
flour to flour fish
minced parsley
lemon wedges

Sprinkle salt inside and outside fish to season it.

Heat skillet with fat; in meantime dip fish in milk, then flour them lightly, put them into hot skillet, sauté until nicely browned, reduce heat if necessary. Brown other side gently, add a little more fat if necessary. Test with fork whether fish is cooked, being careful not to overcook, as they will be dry. Season with pepper, wipe any fat off, serve on heated plates garnished with minced parsley and lemon.

203

Broiled Fish

cooking time about 9 min

utensils
   broiler
serves 2

2 fish or filets (mackerel, red snappers, pompano, trout, croakers, flounder, or other small fat fish)
2 tbsp melted butter or margarine
1 tsp salt per fish
pepper to taste

Sprinkle salt on fish, let marinate in refrigerator about 15 min, brush with melted butter, broil 2-3 min to brown, then lower to finish broiling, baste with butter. If fish is thick, turn over and broil other side. Fish broil very quickly; a filet usually takes about 7 or 8 min. It is best to "stand by" when broiling fish to remove it the minute it is cooked but still juicy.

Serve on heated plates, add wedge of lemon, some minced parsley; a perfectly broiled fish is a perfect delight.

For a basting sauce that is quite good, mix 2 tbsp melted butter with ¼ tsp ginger, ¼ tsp dry mustard, ¼ tsp paprika, and ½ tsp flour. This doesn't alter the taste of the fish but brings out the good fish taste.

Tuna Fish in Shell

broiling time 2-4 min

utensils
   mixing bowl
   4 shells or individual shallow baking dishes
serves 4

1 (7-oz) can tuna fish, drained
½ stalk celery, grated
¼ cup whipping cream
2 tbsp butter or margarine
grind of pepper
squeeze of lemon

Mix ingredients except butter lightly. Pile in shells, dot with butter, squeeze of lemon, broil 2-4 min, browning nicely but being careful not to burn tops.

Filet of Flounder
Stuffed with Crabmeat

cooking time 15-20 min

heatproof baking dishes
6 inches across, 1 inch
deep
mixing bowl
serves 4

1 filet of flounder, cut in portions to fit the
baking dishes
softened butter to smear dishes
½ can lump crabmeat picked over and
shells removed
6 tbsp heavy cream
½ cup unsweetened mayonnaise
butter to dot crabmeat before baking
pepper to taste
sprinkle of paprika

Cut filet in portions to fit baking dishes. Sprinkle ½ tsp
salt on each portion and refrigerate 15 min.

Fit filets in baking dishes, grind a little pepper over them.
Stir cream into mayonnaise, gently mix into crabmeat, spoon this over filet, dot with butter, sprinkle
with paprika, add grind of pepper, bake 15-20 min
until flounder is cooked but juicy and top is golden
brown.

Hot Salmon
in a Jiffy

cooking time 5-10 min

utensils
2 individual small heat-
proof dishes
serves 2

1 (7¾-oz) can of salmon
about 4 heaping tbsp sour cream
3 tbsp milk

Spoon sour cream thinned with milk over salmon, broil
on second shelf from heat, until it is bubbly and
browned, which takes about 5-10 min.

You can vary this by grating a little onion over
salmon before adding sour cream or by squeezing
some lemon juice over salmon or a little wine
vinegar. You can pretty up sour cream with a
sprinkle of paprika.

205

Fried Fish, Southern Style

cooking time about 10 min

utensils
  skillet
  draining rack
serves 2

2 croakers, porgies, small bass, small flounders, butter fish or Norfolk spots
½-1 tsp salt for each fish
⅓ cup white cornmeal
vegetable shortening and 1 heaping tbsp butter to make 1 inch of fat in skillet
pepper to taste
1 tbsp minced parsley
¼-½ lemon for each fish

Dip fish, seasoned with the salt in cornmeal, place in hot fat on medium heat. Don't put fish in until you have tested fat by seeing if a piece of bread comes to the surface instantly and starts browning. Fry fish to a golden brown, don't crowd. Drain on paper towels on rack so the bottom side will not sweat, but will remain crisp. Sprinkle pepper on, garnish with parsley, serve lemon. *"Cucumber Salad" (see its recipe) is delicious served with this.

There are two important things to remember when frying fish: do not overcrowd, and serve as soon as fried. Fried fish is like love; when it cools off, it is no good.

Maria's Two-Ways Fish, Fried or Broiled

cooking time 10-30 min

utensils
  skillet and lid
portions as many as you like

fish filets or small whole fish
enough lemon juice to flavor fish mixed
  with water to cover fish
oil to marinate fish
salt
flour to flour fish
egg, with little salt added, beaten slightly
crumbs to dip fish in

Soak fish in lemon juice and water to cover for about 15 min, wipe, marinate it in oil and salt, turning so that both sides marinate in oil ½ hr before frying or broiling.

Before frying, wipe fish, dip it in flour, then egg, then crumbs. Preheat skillet and brown, reduce heat to low, put lid on and steam-fry until done. A filet may take 5-10 min and a whole fish 15-30 min depending on size. This fish can also be broiled, lowering fish to keep from burning and drying out. This is a man's fish—crusty on the outside, tender on the inside.

Salmon Croquettes

cooking time a few min

utensils
  skillet
serves 2 or 3

1 (7-oz) can salmon with juice
1 slice bread, day-old preferred
1 tbsp grated onion
1 egg mixed with fork
enough vegetable shortening with 1 tsp of
  butter to cover skillet about ¼ inch
¼ lemon to garnish

Tear bread into pieces, add to salmon and its juice, add onion and egg, mixing lightly with 2 forks. Drop with spoon into hot fat on medium heat, brown nicely on both sides, being careful that croquettes don't become dry. Garnish with lemon.

CANNISTER PITCHER. There is no cannister easier to handle than this. It is very inexpensive, easy to grip; the handle saves dropping. These cannisters are quiet to use. You can buy them in different colors, one for sugar, one for flour, etc. They can be bought at all 5 & 10¢ stores, supermarkets, department stores and hardware stores. Besides being easy to clean, they save time and money.

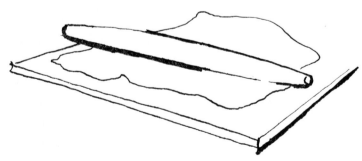

ROLLING PIN. If you plan to make pies or cookies, this is a good rolling pin to have.

Never-fail Single Piecrust

baking time 10-12 min
preheat oven 425°

utensils
mixing bowl
board
rolling pin
pie plate

1 cup unsifted all-purpose flour
½ tsp salt and
¼ tsp baking powder
2 tbsp softened, room temperature butter
   (don't substitute margarine)
2 tbsp vegetable shortening
3 tbsp strained orange juice
flour to roll crust on board

Mix softened butter and vegetable shortening into flour mixed with salt and baking powder, being careful to leave some of the fat, size of peas, for added flakiness.

Stir in orange juice. Make into ball and knead for 1-2 min. Place in refrigerator 1 hr or more, or it can be used immediately.

Roll on floured surface, from center out, not quite to ends as this will thin ends too much. As you roll, lift dough over rolling pin, making sure it does not stick. Do not sprinkle flour on top of dough, flour rolling pin lightly if necessary. This dough does not stick like other doughs. Continue until crust is right size, rolling ends last. Roll crust over rolling pin and unroll onto pie plate.

Shape into pie plate without stretching, as it will shrink when baked if you do. Trim off excess dough with sharp knife.

Punch holes with fork tines all over bottom and sides, being careful not to tear crust. This keeps crust from ballooning up when it is baked without a filling.

Bake 10-12 min in preheated 425° oven. Don't let it burn.

209

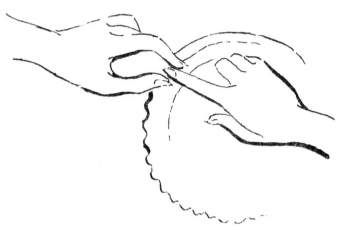

MAKING SCALLOPS ON PIECRUST. These are easy to make and decorative. Make scallop by using thumb and forefinger pushing against forefinger of other hand.

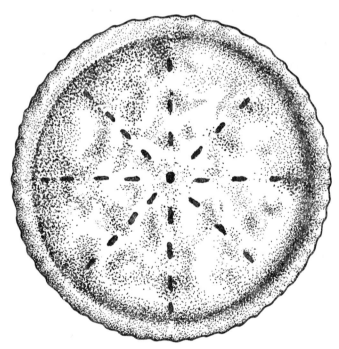

HOW TO SLIT PIECRUST. These slits permit steam to escape and also act as guide in cutting pie.

Never-fail
Double Piecrust

utensils
  mixing bowl
  board
  rolling pin
  pie plate

2 cups unsifted all-purpose flour
1 tsp salt
½ tsp baking powder
¼ cup softened, room temperature butter
  (don't substitute margarine)
¼ cup vegetable shortening
¼ cup strained orange juice
2 tsp melted butter to brush on top pie crust and brush bottom pie crust to keep from getting soggy
flour to roll crust on board

Mix softened butter and shortening into flour mixed with salt and baking powder, being careful to leave some of the fat, size of peas, for added flakiness. Stir in orange juice. Make into 2 balls and knead for 1-2 min. Place in refrigerator 1 hr or more. This helps to make crusts flakier, although it can be used immediately and is very good.

Roll on floured surface 1 ball at a time, roll from center out, not quite to ends as this will thin ends too much. As you roll, lift dough over rolling pin. Make sure it doesn't stick. Do not sprinkle flour on top of dough; flour rolling pin lightly instead. This dough does not stick like other doughs. Continue until crust is the right size, rolling ends last. Roll the crust over rolling pin and unroll onto pie plate. Shape into pie plate without stretching as this causes shrinkage when baked.

Brush one tsp melted butter on bottom of piecrust; this is your insurance for a non-soggy crust. Place it in refrigerator until butter hardens. In meantime, make filling and set aside.

Roll out other ball of dough to make top crust, using same procedure as you did for bottom crust. Place filling in bottom crust, unroll top crust on it. Cut off extra dough. Press edges of both crusts together with tines of fork, or make a fancy design using your index finger to make the indentation, and your thumb and index finger of your other hand to make the scallop around your finger.

For fruit or berry pie be sure to cut slits for steam to escape. Slits have the added advantage of acting as guide to cutting pie. Brush pie with melted butter for a browned crust.

211

fix ahead; freezes fine

Foolproof Shells
for Tarts and Hors d'Oeuvres

baking time 3-5 min
preheat oven 425° for
unfilled shells, 400° for
filled shells

*1 "Never-Fail Double Piecrust" (see its
recipe)

utensils
little tart pans, different
shapes for hors d'oeuvres
larger tart pans for fruit
tarts
cooky sheet
makes about 25 small tarts

The wonderful thing about this recipe is that no matter how
much you handle this crust, it is still tender and flaky and
always comes out perfect. It is a never-fail crust that is very
easy to make.

Make crust; refrigerate until ready to use. Roll out a
little piece at a time and put into tart pan, press-
ing a little bit. Punch holes all over with sharp
prongs of fork. Continue until all are made—rather
tedious work but worth it. Place tart pans on
cooky sheet in preheated 425° oven. Bake about
3-5 min but be careful they don't brown too much.
Cool on rack and remove from tart pans. Let tarts
cool, then stuff with cold filling.

Cold fillings may be *"Creamed Chicken or Chicken
à la King" (see its recipe), or chopped chicken in
thick cream sauce, seasoned with either white wine
or dry sherry, a little pimento or mushrooms or
chopped nuts, or finely chopped scallions.

Another cold filling may be a can of Campbell's frozen
shrimp soup, defrosted, about ½ cup thick cream
shaken with 2 tbsp flour and 4 tbsp dry sherry
and mixed with shrimp soup. Bring to boil, reduce
to low and heat for about 5 min until sauce becomes thick. Let cool before spooning into tarts.
These are delicious eaten cold or hot. They can
be heated in 400° oven 3 min.

212

You can substitute tuna fish for chicken in our "Creamed Chicken" recipe.

Crab meat in thick cream sauce with drop or two of tabasco and sherry or Worcestershire sauce is excellent.

You can freeze tarts stuffed or just the shells to have ready when you need them. The filled tarts can be heated frozen in a 400° oven 5-10 min.

Blueberry tarts are wonderful, made very easily and taste quite "French" when you use 1 box frozen sweetened blueberries. Defrost in strainer to separate juice. The proportion is ½ cup juice, 2 tsp cornstarch, 2 tbsp lemon juice to taste, ¾ cup blueberries. There is about 1½ cups berries and ½ cup juice to a box. Mix cornstarch into juice until it is dissolved and add lemon juice. Bring to boil, then reduce heat until sauce is clear and thick, which takes about 5 min. Pour the sauce over blueberries and let them get cold before spooning into tarts. Serve at once or refrigerate until ready to use.

There is one trick to making this sauce foolproof. Always add cornstarch to juice, any kind of juice, but do not put in any frozen or fresh fruit as it cooks and adds more juice to sauce, which ruins thickening and keeps sauce from getting properly thick. If you are using fresh fruit, make some juice out of part of it or use canned fruit juice, such as pineapple, cherry or whatever you need.

Strawberry tarts can be made the same way, using fresh strawberries as the fruit and frozen strawberries, cooked up into a juice and strained, to be used as the above blueberries were used. The juice so cooked makes a nice shiny glaze.

You can make a different kind of glaze for blueberries, strawberries, bananas or whatever by melting currant jelly and pouring over the fruit, chilling until jelly congeals. You can also use apricot preserves, mashing through a strainer and heating as you did with the currant jelly.

Rosa's Old-fashioned Piecrust

baking time for 1 crust 10-12
min, for 2 crusts about
30 min
preheat oven 425°

utensils
large mixing bowl
large metal spoon
small bowl
rolling pin
board
pie plate
cooling rack

1 CRUST
¾ cup all-purpose unsifted flour
¼ tsp salt
⅓ cup vegetable shortening
3 tbsp iced water
flour to flour board
1 tsp melted butter to brush bottom crust
2 CRUSTS
1½ cups flour
½ tsp salt
⅔ cup vegetable shortening
6 tbsp iced water
flour to flour board
1 tsp melted butter

Use ice cold water or put ice and water in small bowl to get very cold water.

In the large bowl gradually stir iced water into the shortening until it doesn't "take" any more, start stirring in some of the flour mixed with salt, adding rest of water and flour until all has been added. Use your hand to finish mixing, knead for 1 min, don't handle too much. Shape into ball, place in refrigerator for a few hr if you have time for a more tender crust.

Place dough on floured board, flour rolling pin, start rolling, being careful to roll from the middle out, not quite to the ends, as this will thin the ends too much. As you roll, lift dough over rolling pin, put a little flour under dough, so it doesn't stick. Do not sprinkle flour on top of dough, but you can, when necessary, flour rolling pin. Continue until crust is right size, rolling the ends last. Roll crust over rolling pin and unroll on pie plate.

Shape into pie plate without stretching, as it will shrink when baked if you do. Trim off excess dough.

Punch holes with fork tines all over bottom and sides, being careful not to tear crust. This keeps crust from ballooning up when it bakes without a filling.

If you plan to fill the crust immediately and add a top crust, as for apple or peach pie, then don't punch holes in.

If making a 1-crust pie with filling, such as custard, that tends to make the crust soggy, brush bottom crust with 1 tsp melted butter.

For a 1-crust pie, bake 10-12 min, watching to see that the crust doesn't burn.

Cool before adding cold filling, as in lemon meringue pie.

When making a 2-crust pie, roll out 1 crust, place in pie plate, brush 1 tsp melted butter to keep bottom from getting soggy, place in refrigerator for butter to harden.

Roll out the top crust, prepare whatever filling you wish, put filling in bottom crust, moisten edges with a little cold water, put top crust on quickly, press edges together with tines of fork.

Cut slits in top crust to vent steam and to keep crust crisp. See accompanying illustration. The slits act as a guide line when you cut the pie.

Put foil around the edge of the crust to keep edge from burning. The edge crust will brown well under foil.

Bake in preheated 425° oven about 30 min.

Remove to a rack to cool.

fix ahead

Fresh Apple Pie

baking time about 40 min
preheat oven 425°

utensils
large bowl
10-inch heatproof pie plate
serves 6-8

*dough for 2-crust "Rosa's Old-fashioned Piecrust" (see its recipe)
about 5 large apples, Stayman winesap or any juicy, tart variety, peeled and sliced
½ cup sugar sprinkled with cinnamon
1 tsp flour
1 tsp lemon juice
butter to dot apples for a richer pie
1 tsp melted butter to brush on bottom crust

Roll out bottom piecrust. Brush with melted butter after placing in pie pan. Place in refrigerator while you peel and slice apples. Mix sugar, lemon juice and flour with apples. Roll out top crust so everything is ready. Place apple mixture into bottom crust; place top crust on, cut slits for steam to escape from top crust. Place in middle rack of oven, bake about 40 min, being careful that edges of crust don't burn; cover edges with foil if necessary before baking.

This apple pie is delicious served hot.

Lemon Meringue Pie

cooking *time* about 30 min
   preheat oven 425° for
   crust, 350° for meringue

utensils
   large mixing bowl
   saucepan
   rotary beater
   9-inch heatproof pie plate
serves 6-8

*1-crust "Rosa's Old-fashioned Piecrust"
   (see its recipe)
1⅓ cup sugar
3 tbsp cornstarch
4 egg yolks mixed with fork
1 lemon rind, grated
¼ cup lemon juice, strained
1½ cups boiling water
4 egg whites, set aside for meringue
3 tbsp sugar, set aside for meringue

Mix sugar and cornstarch in saucepan, stir in egg yolks, lemon juice and grated lemon rind, gradually stir in the boiling water, bring to boil on high heat. Reduce heat to low, stir, cook 4 min. Remove from heat, let cool. When mixture cools, it thickens. When cold, place in prebaked cold piecrust.

Preheat oven 350°

In large mixing bowl, beat egg whites with rotary beater until soft peaks form. Add sugar, and continue beating until whites are stiff and shiny. Spoon egg whites onto filling, being careful not to leave any space between whites and crust. Do not smooth meringue, let stay in peaks. Place in oven 15 min until meringue is golden brown.

Pumpkin Pie

baking *time* 35 min
   preheat oven 425°

utensils
   large bowl
   small bowl
   9-inch glass pie plate
   rolling pin
   3-qt saucepan
   rotary beater
   wooden spoon
   board to roll dough

*dough for "Never-fail Single Piecrust" (see its recipe)
1 tsp melted butter to brush on piecrust
1 cup canned, unseasoned pumpkin (Libby's is good)
1 tbsp flour
¼ cup honey
½ cup brown sugar
½ tsp salt
5 large eggs
1½ cups milk
½ cup heavy whipping cream
1 tsp nutmeg
½ tsp each cinnamon, ground allspice, ginger, cloves
3 tbsp light rum or brandy

Make dough for pie crust, place in pie plate, brush with melted butter on bottom of crust. Tear a thin strip of foil, put around edge of piecrust to keep it from burning. Place crust in refrigerator while you make filling.

Mix pumpkin, flour, honey, brown sugar and salt together. Add spices. Beat eggs with rotary beater and stir into pumpkin mixture. Stir in the brandy. Boil milk until it comes to top of saucepan, but don't let it boil over. Gradually add to egg mixture, stir in the cream.

Ladle pumpkin mixture into pie shell, sprinkle a little nutmeg on top. Place in preheated 425° oven, bake 10 min. Reduce heat to 350°, bake about 25 min and test by inserting knife in center. If just a little crumb sticks to it, pie is ready.

Blueberry Pie

baking time 30 min
preheat oven 425°

utensils
    large bowl and strainer
    9-inch glass heatproof pie
        plate
serves 6-8

*dough for "Never-fail Double Piecrust"
    (see its recipe)
2 boxes frozen sweetened blueberries, de-
    frosted, drained
2 tbsp flour
juice from ½ lemon
¾ cup sugar
2 tsp melted butter

Make the 2-crust recipe, shape into 2 balls, wrap in saran, chill in refrigerator few hr if there is time.

Roll out 1 ball into crust to fit pie plate, brush with 1 tsp melted butter, put in refrigerator to harden so crust will not get soggy when filled and baked.

Roll out top crust, mix blueberries, flour, sugar and lemon juice, fill bottom crust, moisten edges with a little water, place crust on filling, being careful not to stretch it, cut off excess dough.

Press edges of crusts together with tines of fork to keep juices in. Brush the other teaspoon melted butter on top crust. Make slits to let steam escape when baking. These slits also act as a guide when cutting the pie.

Put foil around edges to keep them from burning, place in middle of preheated oven. Bake 30 min.

This is kind of pie that makes guests clamor for more. This recipe can be used to make any other berry pie.

a quickie

Blueberry Cobbler

cooking time 15-17 min
preheat oven 450°

utensils
    casserole
    mixing bowl

FILLING
1 can Blueberry pie filling
2-3 tbsp lemon juice, depending on filling

DOUGH
1 cup bisquick
¼ cup butter, cut into size of peas
¼ cup milk
butter to smear casserole

To make dough, mix together lightly, being careful to cut the butter into pea size. Set aside a while.

Taste filling mixture to correct seasoning. Heat until hot, place in casserole; with 2 spoons drop in small-size biscuits to cover filling.

Bake in oven 15-17 min until top is a nice brown. Serve hot; the top should be deliciously rich and light and contrast nicely with the tasty filling.

You can make cherry, peach or apple cobblers by using these fillings and you can zip them up with 1 tsp of brandy, preferably the same kind as the fruit used.

fix ahead

Easy Dessert Rolls

baking time 20 min
preheat oven 450°

utensils
mixing bowl
floured board
baking sheet
sharp knife
rubber spatula

ROLL
½ lb softened butter, set aside
1 very large or 2 medium eggs
2½ cups bisquick
1 cup sour cream
1 tbsp sugar
Flour to roll dough

GLAZE
1 egg yolk mixed with 1 tsp water

Mix the bisquick, sugar, sour cream and slightly beaten egg in bowl; knead 1-2 min on floured board until dough is light and puffy. Shape into ball.

With sharp knife, divide dough into halves, continue dividing until you have 8 even pieces. Flour board, so dough will not stick, roll out 1 piece at a time into oblong lengths about 12″ long by 1½″ wide by 1¼″ thick. Place rest of dough in saran in refrigerator until each is needed.

With rubber spatula, brush softened butter on dough, fill center with one of the fillings in the next recipe, fold over to hold in filling. Cut off extra dough at each end and pinch to close.

Place on baking sheet until all are filled. Glaze rolls with egg glaze, bake in preheated oven about 20 min. The rolls will be golden brown and very tasty.

Remove from pan to rack to cool.

The cheese rolls should be eaten the day they are baked. They don't freeze well, but the others freeze fine.

Fillings
for Dessert Rolls

utensils
small bowl

Raisin and Nut Filling (for 1 roll)

1 tbsp melted butter
⅓ cup nuts (preferably pecans), broken into pieces
1 tbsp sugar mixed with ¼ tsp cinnamon

*⅓ cup softened or steamed raisins (see "Steaming" and "Tested Times for Steaming Vegetables")

Mix ingredients together lightly.

Chocolate Nut Filling (for 1 roll)

1 tbsp melted butter
⅓ cup nuts (pecans preferred), broken in pieces
⅓ cup instant chocolate

*⅓ cup softened or steamed raisins (see "Steaming" and "Tested Times for Steaming Vegetables")

Mix ingredients together lightly.

Cheese Filling (for 2 rolls)

1 pkg (7½-oz) farmer's cheese or cottage cheese, drained
1 tbsp melted butter
1 egg yolk
2 tbsp sugar

*⅓ cup softened or steamed raisins (see "Steaming" and "Tested Times for Steaming Vegetables")
2 tbsp bread crumbs
salt to taste

Mix farmer's cheese and butter together; stir in remaining ingredients.

Marmalade or Apricot Jam Filling (for 1 roll)

1 tbsp melted butter
⅓ cup jam or marmalade (Dundee's or Chiver's marmalade are good; Kraft's apricot is good)
1 tbsp sugar mixed with ¼ tsp cinnamon

⅓ cup nuts broken in pieces
⅓ cup steamed raisins (see "Steaming" and "Tested Times for Steaming Vegetables")

Mix ingredients together lightly.

Fresh Apple or Peach Roll

baking time 40 min
   preheat oven 450°

utensils
   10" x 6½" rectangular
      fireproof dish
   screw-top jar

*dough for 1-crust "Rosa's Old-Fashioned
   Piecrust" (see its recipe)
4 cups fresh apples or peaches, peeled,
   sliced into ¼" slices
1 tbsp flour to mix with fruit
¼ cup sugar to taste for apples or peaches
1 tsp sugar for crust
1 tbsp softened butter to spread on dough
1 tsp softened butter to dot rolls
⅔ cup canned apple or peach juice
1 tbsp flour for juice
Butter to butter baking dish
1 tsp sugar to sprinkle over cut pieces of
   fruit roll

Butter baking dish.

Mix fruit, sugar and flour together.

Roll out piecrust dough into an oblong roll 10" by 12",
   spread ½ tsp softened butter over roll. Sprinkle
   1 tsp sugar over roll and lay fruit in center of roll,
   full length. Bring the two sides of roll to middle
   and close.

Cut with sharp knife into 5 pieces. Place each piece
   in baking dish and sprinkle 1 tsp sugar on top
   of rolls; dot with rest of softened butter. If easier,
   place roll in baking dish and then cut into 5 pieces.

Shake the fruit juice and 1 tbsp flour to combine. Pour
   around the rolls, but do not cover rolls with juice.
   Bake in 450° oven for 40 min. Serve warm.

Easy, Delicious Canned Apricot Rolls

baking time 45 min
  preheat oven 450°

utensils
  large mixing bowl
  oblong baking dish 12"
    x 9"
  strainer
  bowl
  rolling pin
  wide spatula
makes 4 portions

*1-crust "Rosa's Old-fashioned Piecrust"
  (see its recipe)
Softened butter to butter baking dish
1 No. 2½ can firm apricots, drained and
  seeded
1 tbsp butter to dot crust roll
1 tbsp butter to dot completed roll
1 tsp sugar
1 tbsp flour

Butter baking dish.

Roll out piecrust dough on floured board until it is
  12" by 9". Dot with 1 tbsp softened butter. Taste
  apricots and add sugar as needed.

Place apricots in center of crust. Bring long sides together, overlapping, and seal. Cut any extra crust
  off ends. Divide roll into 4 portions and place in
  baking dish. Dot rolls with butter and sprinkle
  with 1 tsp sugar. It may be easier to put roll
  into baking dish and cut it there, then proceed as
  above.

Stir flour into apricot juice. Pour around rolls, being sure
  that tops of rolls are not covered so that crusts will
  brown nicely.

Place in preheated oven and bake 45 min.

You can make this out of peaches or cherries; they're equally good.

224

One-Dish Jelly Roll

baking time 12 min
  preheat oven 375°

utensils
  electric mixer or rotary beater
  jelly roll pan, 15½" x 10½" x ¾"
  waxed paper
  cloth towel
makes 1 large thick jelly roll or 2 thin ones

*"Cooked Dried Apricots for Jelly Rolls" (see its recipe) or 1 cup apricot preserves
¾ cup flour
1 tsp baking powder
¼ tsp salt
4 egg whites from extra large eggs
½ cup sugar
4 egg yolks
grated rind of 1 lemon
juice of 1 lemon
½ cup 4X or 10X sugar

Place waxed paper on jelly roll pan, set aside.

Sift together flour, salt and baking powder, set aside.

In large bowl of electric mixer or by hand, beat egg whites stiff on high speed. Gradually add sugar, continue to beat, gradually add egg yolks that have been broken up with fork, beating until thick and yellow, about 3 min. Add lemon juice, then lemon rind, reduce speed to medium and gradually add flour mixture until all has been added.

Pour mixture into baking pan, bake 12 min on medium shelf in the oven. Sprinkle 4X or 10X sugar on towel, turn jelly roll over from pan onto towel, remove waxed paper, cut off any hard crusts. Roll up in towel lengthwise. Cool. Unroll, spread filling on jelly roll, and roll up in towel again. Let stand about 10 min to keep the rolls' shape.

If you prefer a thinner roll, divide the batter into halves, and bake each half only 9 min.

You can vary taste of jelly roll by substituting vanilla for lemon and using strawberries for a filling or whatever jelly or jam you prefer. Fresh strawberries sugared and whipped cream make a deluxe filling as does whipped cream flavored with rum.

The teflon jelly roll pans are fine, but we are like the man who wears a belt and suspenders; we use the wax paper anyhow. We also find we do not have to butter the pans when using wax paper; our jelly rolls do not stick to the pans when we use unbuttered waxed paper. A good commercial apricot preserve can be used instead of the cooked dried apricots.

Cooked Dried Apricots
for Jelly Rolls

cooking time 30 min

utensils
saucepan
metal spoon

1 lb dried apricots
2 cups water
5-6 tbsp sugar to taste

Bring apricots and water to boil. Reduce heat to simmer for 30 min, stirring now and then so apricots do not stick.

Add sugar to taste, bring back to boil, taste and correct if necessary. Boil 1 min.

Stir and mash with metal spoon so that it is spreadable or push through a sieve. Cool.

Chocolate Roll, Tel Aviv Style

baking *time* about 12 min
preheat oven 400°

utensils
electric mixer, rotary beater or wire whip
11" x 16" jelly roll pan
cooling rack
dish towel
wax paper
makes 1 roll

5 large egg whites
⅔ cup sugar
5 large egg yolks
3 tbsp cocoa
vegetable shortening to grease roll pan
confectioners' sugar to sprinkle on towel

Grease pan, put wax paper on, grease again and lightly flour.

Beat the egg whites stiff until they form soft peaks, gradually add sugar and beat until stiff but not dry. This takes about 5 min. You can test by holding up beaters; if egg whites hold their peak, they are ready.

Gradually add egg yolks, broken up with fork, last; sift cocoa over mixture and fold in.

Spread on pan and bake 12 min, cool on rack. Sprinkle towel with confectioners' sugar, turn roll out, peel paper off. Roll up in towel for about 10 min. Unroll, spread with sweetened whipped cream.

Roll up sidewise, the long way, into a thin long roll. Place in refrigerator. Cut with sharp knife that has been moistened.

with a difference

Brandy Pound Cake

baking time 45 min
preheat oven 350°

utensils
electric mixer (optional)
2 tube pans, 8" x 3"
cooling rack
makes 2 cakes

your favorite yellow cake mix
butter to smear pans
flour to flour pans
4 extra large or 6 regular eggs
½ cup whipped butter at room temperature
or soft margarine
¾ cup water
¼ cup brandy
1 cup white or California seedless raisins

Prepare tube pans by buttering and flouring.

Mix all the ingredients together except raisins, beat 4 min in electric mixer or by hand. Stir in raisins. They will go to the bottoms of the cakes when baked, which is fine, as you will serve the cakes bottom up, and they will be decorated with the raisins. Divide batter into 2 tube pans, bake 45 min.

Place on rack to cool 10 min, turn out, being careful to loosen cakes. You can vary this cake by substituting nuts for raisins and you can use loaf pans to bake in if you wish.

Sour Cream Cake

baking time 45 min
preheat oven 325° (glass dish); 350° (aluminum pan)

utensils
9" x 13" cake pan, glass or aluminum
electric mixer (optional)
makes 1 cake

grated rind from 1 orange
1 tsp baking soda stirred into 2 cups sour cream
1 box yellow cake mix
2 large eggs
butter to grease baking dish
a little flour to dust over

Combine cake mix with sour cream mixture, and grated rind; add eggs and mix on high speed 4 min.

Pour into greased, floured baking dish, bake 45 min. Insert toothpick; if it comes out clean, cake is finished. This cake must be baked 45 min without looking.

Old-fashioned
Sliced Almond Cake

baking time about 20 min
preheat oven 375°

utensils
large bowl
baking sheet
grater
pastry board
wooden spoon
rotary beater

¾ lb softened butter
1 rounded tbsp vegetable shortening
1½ cups sugar
2 tsp vanilla
2 tbsp grated orange peel
8 eggs, whites separated from yolks, one
    yolk set aside to make glaze
¼ tsp cinnamon
1 cup blanched sliced almonds
1 cup seedless raisins, steamed (see "Steam-
    ing" and "Tested Times for Steaming
    Vegetables")
4 cups unsifted all-purpose flour
4 tsp baking powder
¼ tsp salt
1 cup flour to shape cakes in

Blend softened butter, vegetable shortening, with sugar.
Do not use an electric mixer. Sprinkle grated orange
peel and vanilla over sugar-shortening mixture.
With wooden spoon, gradually stir in egg yolks,
raisins and almonds.

With rotary beater, whip egg whites until they stand in
peaks, fold whites into batter, then gradually add
flour, sprinkling baking powder and the salt over it.

Put cup of flour in center of pastry board, with wooden
spoon, place small amount of batter on flour.
Shape into a small roll 4 inches long and 2 inches
wide, using your hands. Place on baking sheet.
Continue until all have been shaped and placed
on the baking sheet.

Make glaze with the set aside egg yolk, ¼ tsp cinnamon, 1 tsp sugar and 1 tsp water. Brush this glaze
on rolls.

Bake about 20 mins in preheated oven. Cool and slice.
The baking sheet need not be buttered.

These cakes freeze well; leave them uncut.

229

light and moist

Old-fashioned Sponge Cake

baking time 1 hr
preheat oven 325°

utensils
electric mixer, rotary beater, or wire whip
round tube pans 9" x 3½"

1 tsp flour for coating tube pan
6 very large or 8 medium eggs, separated
¼ cup all-purpose flour placed on wax paper
¼ cup potato starch, placed on top of flour
1 cup sugar
grated rind from 1 lemon
¼ cup strained lemon juice

Coat tube pan with tsp flour by shaking it around in pan.

Separate whites of eggs from yolks, being careful not to get any yolks in the whites. Put yolks in small bowl and whites in large bowl of mixer.

Mix the yolks with spoon for just a second. We have tested and found it unnecessary to beat the yolks a lot.

With spoon mix flour and potato starch together, which also takes only a second.

The method of making this cake is a continuous one, so have all the ingredients ready at hand. Start mixer on high speed and continue until cake is finished.

Beat whites of eggs until stiff and they hold their shape when you lift beaters out (takes about 3½ min).

A spoonful at a time, gradually add sugar, shaking sugar in until all has been added.

With spoon pour a little of the yolks in until all have been added.

Gradually spoon grated rind over batter, and, using a spoon, gradually sprinkle lemon juice over batter.

230

With dry spoon, a little at a time, add flour mixture, shaking spoon to add flour mixture until all has been added.

Stop mixer, pour batter into tube pan, turning pan until all batter is in.

Place in center of preheated oven, bake 1 hr. Do not open oven during baking and do not jar.

Remove from oven to a place free of drafts, turn pan upside down on its legs, let the cake get perfectly cold. The cake should not be jarred while cooling. Beware of slamming doors!

When it is entirely cold, which takes about 2 hrs, remove with spatula and you will have the most delicious moist sponge cake you ever ate.

This cake sounds difficult to make, but it is really very easy to do. It freezes well, and if served with strawberries and whipped cream on the side, it is heavenly.

Lana's Apple Cake

baking time 30-35 min
preheat oven 375°

utensils
mixing bowl
fireproof baking dish, 8½″ x 8½″
spoon
makes 1 cake

1 cup and 2 tbsp bisquick
⅔ cup sugar
⅔ cup thick sour cream with ½ tsp soda added
1 egg, slightly beaten
3 tart juicy apples (like winesap or Stayman)
2 tbsp sugar mixed with ½ tbsp cinnamon
2 tsp butter
butter to butter baking dish

Peel apples, cut into 1/6-inch thick slices.

Mix sugar into bisquick, combine with sour cream and egg. Spoon the batter into buttered baking dish. Arrange apple slices on batter, sprinkle sugar mixture over slices and dot with butter.

Bake 30-35 min in center of oven.

This cake is delicious served warm.

Crème de Cacao
Chocolate Cake

baking time 45 min
preheat oven 350°

utensils
  mixer and big bowl
  2 tube pans, 8" or 8½" x
   3" or 9" x 2¼"
  rubber spatula
  cooling rack
makes 2 cakes

1 (1-lb) box devil's food or chocolate cake
  mix
6 extra large eggs
⅓ cup water
4 tbsp crème de cacao
½ cup butter, softened at room temperature
2 tbsp confectioners' sugar
butter to smear tube pans
flour to sprinkle over pans

Butter and flour both tube pans, shaking out the excess
flour.

Add ingredients to cake mix in the big bowl of your
mixer or mix by hand, four min, stirring carefully
now and then with rubber spatula.

Divide into 2 tube pans. Bake in preheated 350° oven
45 min.

Place on rack to cool 10 min. With spatula or small
knife, loosen cake, remove from pans to cool. This cake is
rich enough to eat "as is" without an icing, and
men especially seem to like this cake.

You can vary this cake by using 4 tbsp Jamaica rum,
which is a rich, sweet rum, instead of the crème de
cacao, for a different taste.

Quick, Easy Lemon Cake

baking time 45 min
    preheat oven 375°

utensils
    electric mixer
    large mixing bowl
    baking dish
serves 6-8

1 pkg yellow cake mix
1 pkg lemon jello
4 eggs
¾ cup cooking oil (Wesson, Kraft, Crisco)
¾ cup water
1 tsp fresh lemon juice
softened butter to grease baking dish

Combine cake mix, lemon jello, eggs, oil, water and lemon juice in bowl of mixer, mix until all ingredients are blended, about 3 min.

Put in greased, floured baking dish and bake 45 min. Test for doneness by inserting toothpick in center of cake; if it comes out clean, the cake is done.

Leave cake in baking dish. This cake is delicious without an icing. However, you can use recipe below to frost cake. Make icing while cake is baking and ice cake while it is still warm.

ICING
1 cup powdered sugar
juice of 1 lemon
2 tsp melted butter

Mix ingredients together until smooth, frost warm cake.

a delicious coffee cake

Grandma Bashe's Bobke

baking *time* about 30 min
  preheat oven 375°

utensils
  large mixing bowl
  wooden spoon
  saucepan
  large tube pan
  cooling rack
serves 12 portions

¼ lb butter
1 heaping tbsp vegetable shortening
1 lb all-purpose flour sifted with ¼ tsp salt
1 cup milk
1½ pieces fresh yeast
1½ tsp sugar
¾ cup sugar
3 extra large eggs
1 tsp vanilla
*½ box or 1 cup steamed raisins (see "Steaming" and "Tested Times for Steaming Vegetables")
butter to grease tube pan well

Measure flour and sift into bowl; set aside.

Heat milk lukewarm and crumble yeast into it, adding 1½ tsp sugar. Put on side of stove to ferment. If stove is too hot, remove. When yeast starts fermenting, add ¾ cup sugar to the flour and make a well.

Melt the butter and vegetable shortening over low heat and cool quickly. Put the cooled butter into the well and add the eggs, vanilla and the yeast mixture. Mix, gradually stirring in the flour.

Beat thoroughly, beating air in, which takes 10 min. Let rise in warm place, free of drafts, and be careful not to bang anything, including doors.

When it rises to double its size, punch down and beat again thoroughly, which will take 10-15 min. Add raisins. Butter tube pan thoroughly, put in dough, leaving a little bit in mixing bowl to make crumb topping, and set aside in warm place to rise again.

Make crumb topping with handful of sugar, handful of flour and ½ cup chopped nuts.

Place crumb topping into bowl with the little bit of dough, crumble all together with your fingers. Sprin-

234

kle this topping over dough. Let dough rise double
in size, then place in middle of oven and bake 30
min.

When done, remove from pan gently, place on rack so
air can circulate around coffee cake. Grandma
Bashe always placed a linen towel on top of a clean
pillow and turned over the bobke on that, so the
precious bobke wouldn't be jarred. Precious little
Grandma! There's no more delicious smell on earth
than a bobke just out of the oven!

Lemon Sponge

baking time 45 min
    preheat oven 350°

utensils
    electric mixer or rotary
      beater
    sifter
    mixing bowl
    7½" heatproof casserole
      (1½ qt size)
    baking pan larger than
      casserole

¼ cup flour
1 cup sugar
¼ tsp salt
1½ tsp grated lemon rind
¼ cup lemon juice
2 beaten egg yolks
1 cup milk
2 egg whites

Sift flour, sugar and salt into mixing bowl. Gradually
stir in lemon rind, lemon juice, egg yolks and milk.
Beat the egg whites stiff, fold them into other
mixture.

Pour into casserole, set in pan with warm water about
1½ inches deep. Bake 45 mins.

Do not open oven door until it is baked, as it will fall
if you do.

Here you have your cake and sauce, too.

Rich Rum Sauce for Cakes

utensils
    electric mixer
makes about 2 cups

1 cup whipping cream
2 large eggs
½ cup sugar
rum to taste

Whip eggs on high speed until they are as thick as whipped cream, beat in sugar.

Whip the cream until thick and fold into whipped eggs, then add rum to taste.

Serve over sponge cake or yellow butter cake, or chill in refrigerator until you are ready for it.

Lemon Sauce

cooking time 5 min

utensils
    heavy saucepan
    wooden spoon

1 cup sugar
2 tbsp cornstarch
1 cup water
juice from 2 lemons

Mix cornstarch into sugar, gradually stir in the water, and the lemon juice. On medium heat stir and boil gently until sauce is clear, which takes about 5 mins. Serve hot.

This sauce can be poured over sponge cake or "Rolled Apple Dumplings" (see its recipe). It can also be used to glaze the "Fresh Apple or Peach Roll" (see its recipe) or the "Easy, Delicious Canned Apricot Rolls" (see its recipe). It is equally good poured over "Sour Cream Cake" (see its recipe) or "Quick, Easy Lemon Cake" (see its recipe).

236

Rich, Thick, Luscious Chocolate Icing

mixing time about 5 min

utensils
electric mixer
wooden spoon
rubber spatula
makes icing for 2-layer cake

3 packages Nestlé's Choco-Bake
1½ cups powdered 10X sugar, sifted
½ cup softened, not melted, butter, room
  temperature
1 tsp vanilla
⅛ tsp salt
1 large egg

Add chocolate to ½ cup sugar and the softened butter,
mixing in mixer or by hand until it is thick, add
the vanilla, salt and then egg and rest of sugar,
mixing until it is very thick, glossy, rich-looking.

You can vary this by adding 1 tsp instant dry coffee to
make a mocha icing.

By adding a teaspoon rum, you will have a different
icing.

*This icing remains as is, without getting hard and dry. It is very smooth,
needs no cooking, and can be made in 5 min.*

Mrs. Gordon's Thimble Butterball Cookies

baking time 12-15 min
    preheat oven 400°

utensils
    plastic thimble
    mixing bowl
    rotary beater
    wooden spoon
    baking sheet with sides

3 egg yolks
¼ cup granulated sugar
8 tbsp softened butter
1 tsp vanilla extract
¼ tsp salt
1⅓ cups and 1 tbsp all-purpose flour
½ cup glazed or maraschino cherries, cut
    in halves

Cream butter and sugar, add egg yolks, vanilla and salt; cream. Gradually stir in flour; the dough should be thick enough to pinch off small pieces and roll into marbles. Place these small balls on cooky sheet.

Make indentation with thimble, in center of each cooky, to flatten it and to put the cherry on.

Bake in middle of preheated oven 12-15 mins.

These cakes eat well and freeze well. The unused whites will come in handy to make "Mrs. Gordon's Cocoanut Kisses" (see its recipe).

Buttery Brandy Cookies

baking time 13 min
    preheat oven 400°

utensils
    large mixing bowl
    flour sifter
    rubber spatula
    electric mixer or wooden
        spoon
    baking sheets
    racks
makes a large batch

¾ cup softened butter
2 cups brown sugar
1 tsp baking soda put in ¾ cup sour cream
2 extra large eggs
¼ cup brandy
1 tsp vanilla
¾ cup milk
3½ cups flour
½ cup potato starch
1 tsp baking powder
¾ tsp salt
1 cup pecans, chopped
*1 cup seedless raisins, steamed plump (see "Steaming" and "Tested Times for Steaming Vegetables")

Sift together flour, salt, potato starch and baking powder; set aside.

Cream softened butter and sugar until smooth and light. Stir in eggs one at a time and mix well. Add flour to the creamed mixture.

Alternately add sour cream and milk to flour mixture until all has been added.

Add vanilla and brandy; last, add nuts and raisins.

With two iced teaspoons, push spoonful of batter onto baking sheet, continue until sheet is full, being careful not to place cookies too close together.

Bake in center of oven about 13 min. Be sure to check oven to see that cookies do not burn.

You can vary these cookies by adding 2 tbsps grated orange peel.

These cookies freeze well.

Sour Cream Cookies

baking time 10-12 min
preheat oven 400°

utensils
  mixing bowl
  wooden spoon
  baking sheet

¼ cup softened butter
1 cup sugar
2 thoroughly beaten eggs
½ tsp soda added to ½ cup sour cream
2 cups flour with ½ tsp nutmeg added
*½ cup raisins, steamed (see "Steaming" and "Tested Times for Steaming Vegetables")
½ cup nuts, chopped
1 tsp vanilla

Mix butter and sugar together until light, stir in eggs, vanilla, add nutmeg-flour mixture alternately with sour cream mixture, then raisins and nuts.

Drop by small spoonfuls on greased baking sheet, bake 10-12 min.

Dorothy's Drop Sugar Cookies

baking time 10-15 min
preheat oven 375°

utensils
  mixing bowl
  baking sheet

1 tsp soda added to 1 cup buttermilk
4 cups all-purpose flour sifted with 1 tsp baking powder and ¼ tsp salt
2 cups white sugar
4 medium-size eggs
¾ cup shortening (½ butter ½ lard)
1 tsp vanilla
1 tsp rum
sugar to sprinkle on cookies

Cream shortening and sugar, blend in eggs, alternately add flour mixture with buttermilk-soda mixture, add vanilla, rum; drop with a teaspoon on baking sheet. Sprinkle sugar on.

Bake in middle of oven. If oven seems too slow, raise to 400°, but be careful not to brown.

240

fix partly ahead

Apple Fritters

cooking time 15-20 min

utensils
skillet
racks
tongs
slotted spoon
serves 6-8

4-6 golden delicious, winesap, mackintosh or other tasty apples, cored, peeled and sliced into thin rings
sugar, if necessary, to sprinkle on apples
orange, pineapple, or lemon juice to pour over apples to keep them from discoloring
tasteless fresh oil, enough to fill skillet about ¾" below top.
powdered sugar

FRITTER BATTER
1 cup all-purpose unsifted flour
½ tsp salt
¼ tsp sugar
2 tbsp melted butter
1 cup milk
2 eggs, yolks separated from whites

Fritter batter is made by mixing all batter ingredients together except whites of eggs, which are whipped stiff and folded in.

Heat oil on high heat, then reduce to medium high. Test with piece of bread by dropping it in. If it rises to top immediately and starts browning, oil is ready.

Dip apple rings in batter about 3 at a time. Lift out with tongs, drop into fat and fry until golden color on one side. Turn on other side and when that is golden color, remove to rack to drain. Remove any particles of batter in oil, as they will burn. Continue until all are fried. Sprinkle powdered sugar on.

Be careful that fat doesn't get too hot. If necessary, these can be made earlier and reheated in pan on rack in 400° oven 3-5 mins.

Banana fritters and pineapple fritters are equally good. You can use canned pineapple rings, draining off juice and letting the pineapple dry.

241

Rolled Apple Dumplings

baking time 25-30 min
  preheat oven 450°

utensils
  mixing bowl
  fireproof baking dish, 12″
    x 7½″
  strainer

FILLING

2 1-lb cans pie-sliced apples (Musselman's
  is fine)
1 tbsp lemon juice, poured over apple
  slices to marinate

SAUCE

4 tbsp sugar mixed with 1 tsp cinnamon
¼ tsp flour
1 tbsp butter
2 cups apple juice
sugar to taste

DOUGH

1 cup bisquick
2 tbsp butter to mix with bisquick
¼ cup milk
flour for board

1 tbsp melted butter to rub over dough
2 tbsp butter to dot apples
1 tbsp softened butter to grease baking
  dish
1 tbsp butter to dot finished roll

To make dough, cut butter the size of peas and sprinkle pieces over the bisquick. Add milk, combine lightly, being careful to leave butter in pieces. Make into ball, flour the board, roll into a rectangular shape, smear the melted butter over dough, refrigerate a few min only to let butter harden.

Strain apples from lemon juice, add lemon juice to apple juice.

Arrange the apples on the dough, sprinkle flour over them, and the sugar-cinnamon mixture, leaving 1 tsp to use later. Dot with butter, roll up like jelly roll. Place in buttered baking dish, seam side down, sprinkle tsp sugar-cinnamon mixture on top, dot with butter. Pour lemon-apple juice with sugar to taste around dumpling, but be careful that juice does not cover dumpling, and bake 25-30 min. Baste dumpling with apple juice after it has baked 15 min, continue baking until done. Serve hot.

This dumpling reheats fine. You can make it one day, refrigerate, reheat the next without any loss of flavor or freshness, but be sure to serve it hot.

You can vary this by using any other fruit; fresh fruit is excellent, only you will have to use canned juice for the sauce.

fix ahead

Royal Sherry
Cake Pudding

cooking time until mixture be-
gins to boil

utensils
strainer
glass baking dish 8" x 4"
saucepan

1 box frozen strawberries
1 box Royal custard mix
1 pkg lady fingers or slices of good commercial pound cake
2¼ cups milk
2 tbsp dry sherry
1 tbsp and 2 tsp cornstarch
2 tbsp water

Defrost strawberries (takes about 2 hr), separate from juice with strainer. You will have ¾ cup juice. Don't use strawberries in this recipe.

Arrange half of lady fingers or pound cake on bottom of dish (you can even use an aluminum foil dish). Sprinkle over them 1 tbsp sherry (an empty liquid Sucaryl bottle is a handy thing to keep for sprinkling liquids). Set aside.

Make the Royal custard according to directions on box. Pour about half over lady fingers, let cool in refrigerator until it sets, make glaze of strawberry juice in meantime by mixing it with 1 tbsp and 2 tsp cornstarch mixed with 2 tbsp water, placing on heat, stirring, cooking until glaze becomes clear and thick. Spoon on top of custard, repeat with layers, again letting custard set. Place in refrigerator until ready to serve, unmold, slice.

fix ahead

Orange Cake Pudding

baking time 50 min
  preheat oven 325°

utensils
  7½" x 3" fireproof un-
    covered baking dish
  large mixing bowl
  saucepan
  steamer
  rotary beater
  cooling rack

butter to butter casserole
2 cups orange cake, cubed
4 large eggs
¼ cup sugar
2 cups milk
½ cup Grand Marnier
*½ cup white raisins, steamed (see "Steam-
    ing")
¼ tsp salt

Butter casserole and set aside. Beat eggs with rotary
  beater, mix in sugar, salt, gradually add the Grand
  Marnier.

Boil milk until it reaches top of saucepan, but don't let
  boil over, gradually stir into egg mixture, add to
  cubed cake and the raisins.

Ladle pudding into uncovered casserole and bake about
  50 min, test by inserting knife near edge; if clean,
  the pudding is done.

Remove to rack to cool; serve when pudding is cold.

Keep any leftover pudding in refrigerator, as puddings
  are perishable.

Rum or Sherry Cake Pudding

baking time 35-50 min
preheat oven 325°

utensils
rotary beater
large mixing bowl
saucepan
casserole, no cover, 7½"
x 3"

butter to butter casserole
½ cup Bacardi light rum or sherry
5 large eggs
¼ cup sugar
2 cups milk
1 cup raisins
pinch of salt
nutmeg
2 cups coffee cake (Sara Lee's is good),
torn or cut into cubes or small pieces

With rotary beater, beat eggs in large bowl. Add the
sugar, salt, rum or sherry.

Bring milk to boil, let boil but be careful not to let boil
over, gradually stir milk into egg mixture. Lightly
mix in cake pieces, raisins, and ladle pudding mixture into casserole, sprinkle nutmeg over it.

Place in middle of oven, bake 35-50 min, test by inserting knife near edge of pudding; if clean, it is ready.

Cool, keep refrigerated; puddings are perishable.

*This dessert can have two entirely different flavors depending on
whether you use rum or sherry. Lucky New Yorkers can substitute
Dean's rum cake for the coffee cake and rum in this recipe. Dean's
address is 5 E. 54 St., New York, N. Y.*

Plum- or Strawberry-glazed Noodle Pudding

baking time about 45 min
   preheat oven 350°

utensils
   pot
   round fireproof casserole,
     8½" x 3¼"
   rotary beater
   small bowl
serves 6

1 (8-oz) pkg broad noodles
1 pt commercial sour cream
½ lb cottage cheese
¼ cup melted butter
3 extra large eggs or 5 regular eggs
¼ cup sugar to taste
thick yellow plum preserves or strawberry
   preserves
½ tsp salt

For a light pudding do not make early and let sit until you are ready to bake; instead make and bake immediately.

Boil noodles as directed, cook 7 min, run cold water over and drain.

Butter casserole, set aside while you add the melted butter to noodles, stir in sour cream, cottage cheese, salt, sugar, gently.

Fold in the eggs, mixed with rotary beater until light, spoon into casserole. Spoon plum preserves lightly over top. Bake about 45 min.

You can vary this pudding by adding ½ cup white raisins and omitting the plum preserves. You can also slice a tart apple or two and alternate with a layer of the noodles.

CUSTARD PAN. This inexpensive baking pan is excellent for baking custards.

French Caramel Custard

baking time 40-45 min
    preheat oven 325°

utensils
    large saucepan
    rotary beater
    round aluminum cooking
      pan about 9" x 3½"
    wooden spoon
    mixing bowl

2½ cups sugar
8 eggs
1 qt milk
1 tsp vanilla

Heat 2 cups sugar over medium heat, stirring all the while until it becomes liquid, and is caramel-colored. Do not burn. Without burning yourself, swirl it gently over custard baking dish, covering bottom and sides. Set aside to let harden while you prepare the custard.

Beat eggs with rotary beater, add ½ cup sugar and vanilla. Boil milk once until it reaches top of saucepan; don't let it boil over, but be sure to let it boil, not just bring it to boil.

Gradually stir milk into eggs, pour over caramel in baking dish, bake 40-45 min. Test by inserting knife between edge and middle; if it comes out clean, custard is done. Remove from oven.

Place on rack to cool. When completely cold, not before, you can place in refrigerator.

Do not cook custard too long, as it will get watery. You never need to cook custard in a pan of water; our method makes a smooth, delicious custard.

247

Royal Pear Custard Dessert

cooking time a few min
  marinating time 1 hr

utensils
  saucepan
  glass pie plate or individ-
    ual dishes
portions 4-6

1 can large pear halves
kirsch or sherry
1 box Royal custard flavor dessert mix
2¼ cups milk
currant or other jelly

Follow directions on mix. Pour at once into heatproof
  pie plate, or, better still, into individual dishes. Put
  in refrigerator to set.

Drain pears and marinate in kirsch or sherry 1 hr.

Pour off kirsch and save it. Place pears concave side up
  on cold, thick custard; fill each pear with tsp of
  currant jelly and place in refrigerator.

When ready to serve, spoon some of the kirsch over
  this dessert.

fix ahead

Orange Jello Mousse

utensils
    mixing bowl
    mold
serves 6-8

2 pkg orange jello
1 (1-lb) can Monarch light seedless grapes, drained
1 large can mandarin oranges, drained
½ cup sweet orange wine
2 bananas
2 cups water
watercress

    You will have 4 cups liquid with water, wine, canned grape juice, canned mandarin orange juice, bring to boil, stir into jello until dissolved. Spoon some jello into mold, **refrigerate until set**, arrange whatever design you wish, using some of the grapes, oranges, and sliced bananas, spoon some jello to cover, refrigerate until that sets. Continue until all has been used up and refrigerated; the mold is finished when it all sets.

    Unmold by dipping mold a second in hot water; then turn mold upside down on serving plate; the jello mousse comes out easily. Put immediately back in refrigerator until ready to serve. Arrange some watercress around it.

    If you wish, you can use ¾ cup orange wine and reduce other liquid ¼ cup.

Black Cherry Jello Mousse

utensils
    mixing bowl
    mold
serves 6-8

2 packages of cherry jello
2 cups hot water
½ cup Manischewitz sweet concord wine
1 no. 2½ can black seeded cherries, drained
1 cup chopped walnuts

Water, wine and cherry juice will make 4 cups liquid. Dissolve jello in hot liquid. Spoon some of jello into mold, refrigerate until it sets, decorate with the cherries and walnuts, add more jello, refrigerate to set and continue until all has been used up and your mold is set. It should be so arranged that when the mold is removed, the mousse looks very pretty.

To unmold, dip mold in hot water for a second, turn it over onto plate; refrigerate until ready to use.

These can be made in individual molds, too.

Flamed Brandied Peaches

broiling time about 5 min

utensils
  flameproof dish
  small saucepan
  large matches
serves 4 or as many as you
  wish

4 very large canned firm cling peaches,
  thoroughly drained
1 tbsp butter
1 tsp brown sugar
¼ tsp cinnamon
6 tbsp brandy

Buy largest size of better brand of peaches in order to obtain firm fruit.

Sprinkle peach halves with brown sugar in the centers; dot with butter and cinnamon.

Place the dish so that surfaces of peaches are about 4 inches from the hot broiling element. Broil 5 min.

Pour warmed brandy over peaches. Averting your face, ignite the brandy with large match and serve immediately.

a quickie

Flamed Brandied Black Cherries

utensils
  small saucepan
serves 6

1 large can of large, seeded black cherries
about ½ cup brandy or kirsch
vanilla ice cream to serve 6

Place ice cream in pretty, clear bowl.

Heat the brandy or kirsch.

Pour cherries over ice cream, ignite brandy or kirsch and pour over cherries. Serve at once.

This is quite easy to make and luscious to eat.

Fresh Pineapple
à la Waldorf

utensils
   individual glass dessert
   plates
serves about 6

1 fresh, ripe, sweet pineapple
about ½ can cocoanut, fresh or canned, grated or Southern style
about 4 tsp green crème de menthe
1 quart good-quality vanilla ice cream

Peel, slice and cut pineapple into spears or use Dole's canned pineapple spears.

Sprinkle crème de menthe over pineapple, leave in refrigerator for about 2 hr. Do same with cocoanut.

When ready to serve, arrange pineapple spears, spoke-fashion, on dish and place round scoop of ice cream on top, being sure that the pretty green pineapple shows. Spread the top of the ice cream with the green cocoanut.

You can vary by putting maraschino cherries into ice cream before scooping out.

a quickie

Sauced Kadota Figs

serves 4-6

1 large jar large Kadota figs
1 pt sour cream
crème de cacao

The large jars have the largest figs; try to get firm ones, too.

Drain jar of figs. Chill. Combine sour cream with enough crème de cacao to give a light tan tint and a nice cocoa taste.

Pour this over figs.

Glamour Hint on Baked Apples

cooking time 1 hr
  preheat oven 400°

utensils
  glass baking dish
  saucepan
serves 6

6 firm, juicy, large baking apples (Stayman or winesap)
1 (12-oz) jar clear currant jelly
¼ jar water

Core apples and peel them ¾ down, place in baking dish. Cook the jelly and water until jelly dissolves, pour over apples.

Place apples in middle of oven, bake and baste for about 1 hr. When apples are baked and jelly has become a glaze over the apples, they are ready. Be sure to keep spooning jelly over apples as they cook, as this is what glazes them.

Fruit Supreme

utensils
  sherbet glasses
serves as many as you wish

For an appetizer, place sherbet in center of your prettiest sherbet glasses. For a party, arrange either fresh or canned fruit around attractively. Strawberries, raspberries, peaches, cherries, nectarines, apricots and mandarin oranges are fine. Pour a little brandy or kirsch over the fruit. Brandy goes well with peaches and apricots. If using mandarin oranges, dribble orange wine over them. Use as a first course.

For a dessert, substitute a good vanilla ice cream for sherbet. Arrange fresh fruit around it. Make sauce of either frozen raspberries or strawberries by defrosting and pushing through sieve and pouring over cream.

Use fruits in season. Canned fruits are delicious, too, especially if you select firm fruit.

Mrs. Gordon's Cocoanut Kisses

baking time about 18 min
preheat oven 375°

utensils
mixing bowl
double boiler
rotary beater
spoon
baking sheet

softened butter to butter baking sheet
½ cup glazed or maraschino cherries, halved or quartered
1 cup sugar
3 egg whites
1 tsp cornstarch
2 cans moist cocoanut
1 tsp vanilla
grated peel of 1 orange

Beat egg whites until stiff, gradually beat in sugar and stir in cornstarch.

Cook, stir this mixture in double boiler over hot, not boiling, water, until the sugar is dissolved, taste to be sure. Remove from heat, cool slightly.

Add grated orange peel, vanilla, cocoanut, drop with teaspoon onto baking sheet. Decorate with piece of cherry in center of mound.

Bake about 18 min, remove from pan immediately. Cool on wire rack.

If you prefer crisp kisses, keep them thin; a high mound will make the kisses chewy.

The yolks of the eggs can be used to make "Mrs. Gordon's Thimble Butter Ball Cakes" (see its recipe).

good way to use 3 leftover whites

White Raisin
Nut Kisses

baking time 30 min
    preheat oven 225°

utensils
    baking sheets
    waxed paper
    spatula
    mixing bowl
    rotary beater

3 extra large egg whites
1 cup granulated sugar
½ box white raisins
½ lb chopped nuts, pecans preferred
grated rind of 1 California orange

Beat egg whites stiff but not dry. Add sugar by spoonfuls very slowly at first, then continuously at moderate speed into whites, beating until granulated sugar is absorbed. If you can still feel grains of sugar, don't be alarmed—the kisses will be all right. Mix in the rind, nuts and raisins. Drop by small spoonfuls on baking pan.

Bake in preheated oven 30 min and remove at once from the cooky sheet with spatula. Let cool. These freeze fine, and if kept at room temperature, don't place in a well-closed cooky jar. Instead, place in jar with wax paper loosely put on top.

a quickie; can be prepared ahead

Mocha Ice Cream

utensils
metal spoon
small mixing bowl
serves 4

4 cups vanilla ice cream
4 tsp instant coffee

Soften ice cream by mixing slightly. Stir in instant coffee and replace in freezer compartment.

You can vary this by adding ½ cup chopped pecans.

can be prepared ahead

Vanilla Ice Cream Delight

utensils
blender or mortar and pestle

4 cups vanilla ice cream
1 cup peanut brittle

Pulverize peanut brittle in blender or with mortar and pestle. Mix ingredients together; place in freezer compartment until ready to serve.

This can be varied by mixing 2 tsp dry instant coffee to taste, or 1 cup Grape-Nuts cereal to taste, or candied cherries and about 4 tsp kirsch into ice cream.

256